European Civil and Military Clothing

From the First to
the Eighteenth Century

Frederick Stibbert

Dover Publications, Inc.
Mineola, New York

Bibliographical Note

This Dover edition, first published in 2001, is an unabridged reprint of the illustrations in *Abiti e Fogge Civile e Militari dal I al XVIII Secolo*, by Frederick Stibbert, published by Istituto Italiano d'Arti Grafiche, Bergamo, Italy, in 1914. All the captions have been translated into English. A new Preface has been specially prepared for this new edition by Dr. Kirsten Aschengreen Piacenti, Director of the Stibbert Museum in Florence, Italy.

DOVER *Pictorial Archive* SERIES

Library of Congress Cataloging-in-Publication Data

Stibbert, Frederic, d. 1906.
    [Abiti e fogge civili e militari dal I al XVIII secolo. English]
    European civil and military clothing from the first to the eighteenth century/ Frederick Stibbert.
        p. cm. — (Dover pictorial archive series)
    An unabridged reprint of the illustrations in Abiti e fogge civili e militari dal I al XVIII secolo, first published in 1914. All the captions have been translated into English. With new preface. Cf. Bibliographical note.
    Includes bibliographical references.
    ISBN-13: 978-0-486-41748-6
    ISBN-10: 0-486-41748-4 (pbk.)
    1. Costume—Europe—History. 2. Military uniforms—Europe—History. I. Title. II. Series

GT720 .S6813 2001
391'.0094—dc21

2001028620

Manufactured in the United States by Courier Corporation
41748403   2015
www.doverpublications.com

PREFACE
FREDERICK STIBBERT: HIS LIFE AND WORK

On the opening page of an album of watercolor drawings representing sixteenth-century knights and princesses is the following inscription: "F. Stibbert/Original watercolor drawings for his Costume book/1868." Frederick Stibbert (1838–1906) inherited the family fortune in 1859, when he came of age (his father died when he was only four), and he started collecting immediately. The brief comment in his sketchbook, written a few years later, clearly tells us that the intention of compiling a history of costume was at the back of his mind from the very beginning. Indeed, it was probably the inspiration for most of the objects that he was to acquire during the next fifty years.

The project of the history remained vivid throughout his life, as witnessed by the sketchbooks that he gradually filled with drawings drawn from paintings, tomb slabs, monumental sculptures, etc. From 1877 onward he started having the copper plates engraved. He employed three well-known engravers: the Neapolitan Leonardo de Vegni, and from 1887 the Genoese Filippo Livy and Vincenzo Stanghi from Florence. A note "not yet engraved/1899/F.S.," added in pencil to the above quotation, indicates that as late as 1899 this preparatory work had not yet been completed. In his will Stibbert stipulated that his heir, Count Roberto Pandolfini, was to arrange for the publication, and he left 10,000 lire (about $1 million in today's money) specifically for this purpose. In 1914 the first edition of *Abite e Fogge Civili e Militari* (150 copies) was printed by the Istituto Italiano d'Arti Grafiche in Bergamo. By 1937 these were sold out. After the Second World War the local bank, Cassa di Risparmio della Toscana, had a facsimile version made for private distribution. And somewhere along the line an English version was published in the United States.

For many years Stibbert's history, in any language, has been out of print, and it is with great pleasure that the Stibbert Museum greets the present republication. It is not only a tribute to the extraordinary man who was the founder of the museum that bears his name, it is also the surest way to understand the moving spirit of this great collector. Through this volume we apprehend the reason for the long series of sixteenth-century portraits of the Spanish royal family to be found in the museum; the vast collection of arms and armor from Europe, Japan, and the Islamic world; the numerous costume prints and illustrated books in the library; and the garments themselves, including rare examples of Elizabethan doublets and sixteenth-century Venetian shoes. The museum may seem heterogeneous and eclectic at first sight, but there was a unifying vision behind the 56,000 objects that Stibbert left to the city of Florence. This book is the visual expression of his deep interest in the way people moved, dressed, and lived—anywhere, at any time.

Frederick Stibbert was born in Florence, and died there. His father had been a colonel in the Coldstream Guards, his grandfather governor-general of Bengal, India, whence the family fortune originated. His mother was Italian, and it was her villa on the Montughi hill that Frederick, or Federigo, transformed into his museum. Situated in the midst of its own park, surrounded by the olive groves and vineyards of its own farm, it is still a verdant oasis only ten minutes outside hectic Florence. As his collection grew, Stibbert bought an adjacent villa and built a great Knights' Hall to connect the two houses. He further commissioned a façade to serve as the unifying factor of all three elements, and added the large ballroom. His mother's garden was a typical formal Italian giardino that Stibbert turned into a romantic English park, with temples, loggias, cascades, and a little lake where he could boat in the summer.

Though deeply attached to his mother and her native Tuscany, Stibbert was educated in England, at Harrow and later Cambridge, and his years in England as well as the friends he made there were highly influential to his outlook and interests. At the age of twenty one he returned to Italy and for a brief moment took part in the stirring events of the times, serving in Garibaldi's army against the Austrians. He was awarded a medal for military valor, and his name is inscribed on a plaque under the Loggia dei Lanzi, in Florence, which lists the Florentine youths who served with distinction in the Italian War of Independence.

After this brief interlude he dedicated the rest of his life to his collection, which soon took the shape of a museum—"my museum" he called it, "on which I have spent so much care and money." He also kept a careful watch over his inherited fortune, leaving it intact, if not larger, at his death. By about 1880 the museum was already a reality, and Queen Victoria was among the first visitors during her stays in Florence. In 1887, on the occasion of the unveiling of the new façade, Stibbert opened his museum to "all and sundry" for three weeks. The façade was designed in the neo-Gothic style, and three days of medieval pageants were organized to celebrate its completion. There was even a formal ball in the city hall (Palazzo Vecchio), in which Stibbert took an active part. But besides that he evidently felt that his museum was so much in character that it ought somehow to be incorporated in the celebrations.

It was the world of knights and damsels that Stibbert wanted to re-create. His idea was not to collect a series of masterpieces, although he acquired with great acumen. He bought incessantly, spending vast sums to obtain what he wanted. His focus changed over the course of time, but a constant factor remained: the objects had to come to life. The Cavalcades that are still the dominant feature of the museum were created by him with great attention to detail. Down the middle of the Knights' Hall a procession of sixteen mounted knights advance two abreast. Preceded by a herald, four German horsemen in splendid sixteenth-century (called "Maximilian") armor appear; followed by four Italians dressed in armor by some of the most famous masters of the time (e.g., Pompeo della Cesa); succeeded by four Turkish riders of the Ottoman Empire. From above a life-size St. George and the Dragon look down upon them. The horses are all of the proper size and weight, some heavy enough to carry the massive armored Europeans, others light enough to meet the needs of the swift warriors of Islam. Stibbert himself had a large stable and made sure that mistakes were not made in the equine reproduction.

The physiognomy of the knights was also chosen with care: Here walks a German *Landsknecht*, there a Persian foot soldier. A smaller hall, copied from the Alhambra in Spain, houses the Indian Cavalcade, with mounted maharajas and their guards. Yet a third Cavalcade represents Samurai warriors and archers. These "life-size dolls" were executed in Japan in the 1880s and bought by Stibbert together with the Japanese arms and armor on display. Some of the boxes were even found unopened at the time of his death.

Stibbert must be reckoned among the pioneer collectors of Japanese art. The country opened up in 1868, and his earliest purchases are from 1870. He visited the great international exhibition in Paris where Japanese objects were first shown, but the main bulk of the collection was acquired from antique dealers in Florence and London. The collection numbers 1,800 pieces and is considered the largest outside Japan. Stibbert's passion was arms and armor. He began buying soon after the Samurai caste had been abolished and their arms were beginning to come on the market.

He was equally fortunate with his collection of Islamic arms. In the second half of the nineteenth century, when Turkey was modernizing her army, the contents of the St. Irene fortress came up for sale. Stibbert's purchases provided the museum with an extraordinary selection of fine weaponry from the Islamic world.

Although Stibbert traveled widely in Europe and visited London regularly, he only once crossed the Atlantic Ocean and once the Mediterranean. In 1869, in Cairo for the opening of the Suez Canal, he attended the first performance of *Aida*, and ventured as far as Thebes. His sketchbooks are full of impressions of this journey. His most important purchases of Egyptian art, however, preceded this period. "Egyptomania" may in fact be called his first overwhelming interest. As early as 1859 he commissioned a small "Egyptian" temple to be built by his lake, with a procession of little terra-cotta sphinxes leading up to both the front and back entrances. In 1864 he bought two important sarcophagi, one of them complete with mummy, as well as a series of antique bronzes.

Apart from these Egyptian artifacts, the Stibbert collection spans chronologically from the late fourteenth to the mid-nineteenth centuries. Stibbert's last hero was Napoleon. To the emperor's memory he dedicated an entire room, once he had been able to acquire the sumptuous *petit costume* Napoleon wore for his coronation as King of Italy in 1805.

The vast Stibbert Museum building unites the founder's museum and his personal dwelling, including a series of furnished reception rooms and the private rooms on the floor above. The installation in both sections is still of the nineteenth century, largely as Stibbert left it. His vision permeates every corner and hovers over every object. He created it, and through some quirk of destiny it has remained almost unchanged. This is the particular charm of the museum, and visitors soon fall under its spell. However, the very size of the collection and the amassing of objects in the showcases make it difficult to see them all, let alone enjoy them individually.

Today the policy of the museum is to arrange small exhibitions in a separate modernized section of the building. Here, year by year, selections of objects from the main collection are shown and a story woven around them. The most recent was dedicated to Japan ("Dragons and Peonies"). The most popular, "Dress for the Body—Body for the Dress," offered a comparison between European and Middle Eastern ways of dressing from the sixteenth to the nineteenth centuries. The Europeans, in conformity with their robotlike armor, shaped their bodies with corsets and stays to suit their ideals and ethics; their Eastern counterparts were generally willing to let the body be, covering it with loose, highly colorful, voluminous garments. Armor, costumes both European and Eastern, and corroborative paintings and prints all came from the museum itself, as if the idea of the exhibition had already been in the mind of its founder.

Frederick Stibbert was indeed a remarkable figure, even for the second half of the nineteenth century. He had a vision, and he had the means to make his vision a reality. His museum and his monumental book stand as testimonies to his wish to share this with posterity.

Kirsten Aschengreen Piacenti
Director of the Stibbert Museum

1 *England*

1st Century, A.D.

1 A priestess. 2, 5, 12 Warriors. 3 A chief. 4 Bodicea, Queen of the Iceni (d. 61). 6, 7, 8, 9 Priests. 10, 13 Roman citizens of Great Britain. 11 Female figures. 14 A soldier discharged from the British court.

Sources: Meyrick & Smith; Planché; Strutt.

2   *Eastern Empire*

4th, 5th, and 6th Centuries

1 Emperor Justinian I, the Great (d. 565). 2 A gentlewoman. 3 A pope. 4 An emperor.
5 Emperor Theodosius I.

Sources: Hefner-Alteneck (1860 and 1879); Kretschmer, Plate 23.

3   *Eastern Empire*
6th Century

1, 2 The consuls Flavius Felice and Magno. 3 A young girl of the nobility. 4 A Greek doctor.

Sources: 1–3 Ivory tablet in the Cabinet de Médailles, Paris. 4 Miniature in the Imperial Library, Vienna.

4   *Eastern Empire*
6th Century

The Empress Theodora with a retinue from the Imperial Court.

Source: Mosaics of the Church of San Vitale, Ravenna.

5 Eastern Empire

6th, 7th, and 8th Centuries

The Emperors Justinian I, Phocas, and Justinian II; a bishop, a priest, and a soldier of the Imperial Guard.

Sources: Mosaics of the Church of San Vitale, Ravenna, and contemporary codices.

6 *France*

8th Century

1, 2, 3, 4, 5 Churchmen dressed according to the custom of the 8th century. 6 The Emperor Lothario. 7, 8 Warriors. 9 King Charles the Bald. 10 An official of the Court.

Sources: 1–5 Ancient evangelariums in the Musée des Souverains, Paris, and the Abbey of St. Medard, Soissons. 10 Manuscript Bible in the Abbey of St. Martin, Tours.

7   *Anglo-Saxons*

8th Century

1 A stone slinger. 2 An archer. 3 A warrior. 4 A squire. 5 A king. 6 A chief. 7, 8, 9
Minstrels. 10 A juggler. 11, 12, 13 Peasants.

Sources: Ancient Saxon codices; Meyrick & Smith; Strutt.

8   *Anglo-Saxons*

8th, 9th, and 10th Centuries

1, 2, 3 Priests. 4 A gentlewoman. 5 A princess. 6, 7, 8 Feminine attire. 9 A soldier.
10 A prince. 11, 12 Gentlemen. 13 A soldier.

Sources: "Missal of St. Augustine" in the Harleian collection; other codices; Hefner-Alteneck
    (1860); Meyrick & Smith.

9   *Eastern Empire*

9th Century

1 Gregory of Nazianzen. 2. A gentlewoman. 3 A maiden. 4 St. Helen in the garb of an empress. 5 A maiden. 6 A warrior.

Sources: 9th-century codex, transcribed for Basil I, the Macedonian, preserved in the Bibliothèque Nationale, Paris; Hefner-Alteneck (1860).

10 *France*

9th Century

1 A priest. 2 A Frankish priest. 3 A commoner. 4, 5 Gentlewomen. 6, 7 Warriors.
8 A Canon of St. Martin of Tours. 9 A priest. 10 A warrior. 11 Charles the Bald (d. 877).

Sources: Missal in the Treasury of the Cathedral of Metz; old codex in the Royal Library, Brussels;
prayer book in the Musée des Souverains, Paris; Bar; Montfaucon.

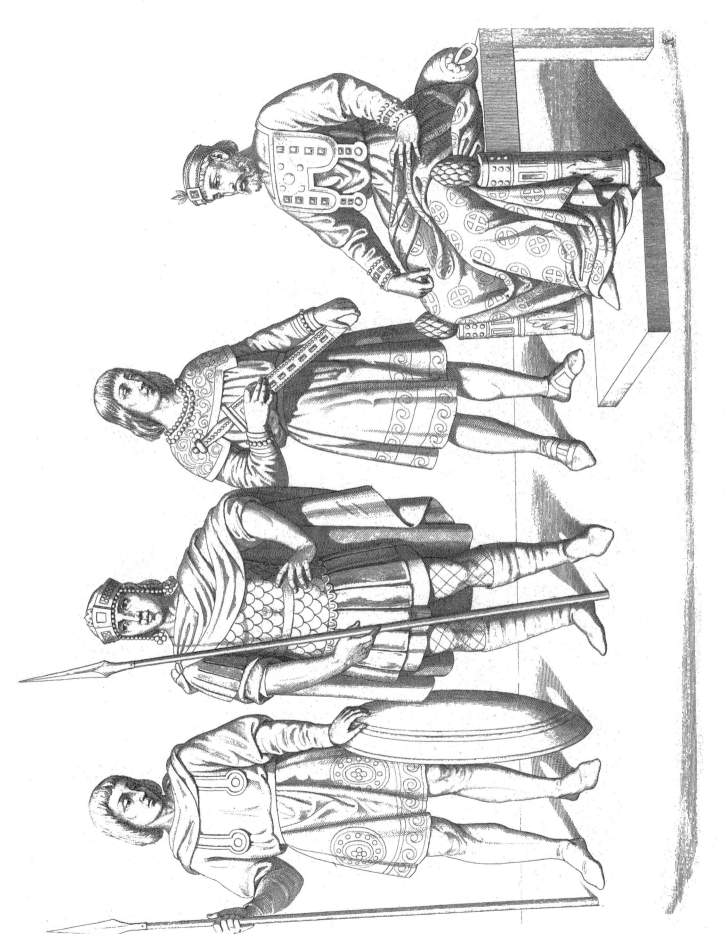

11 *Eastern Empire*
9th Century

1, 2 Soldiers of the Imperial Guard. 3 The "Swordbearer" of the Emperor. 4 Emperor
Basil I, the Macedonian.

Sources: Hefner-Alteneck (1860); Kretschmer.

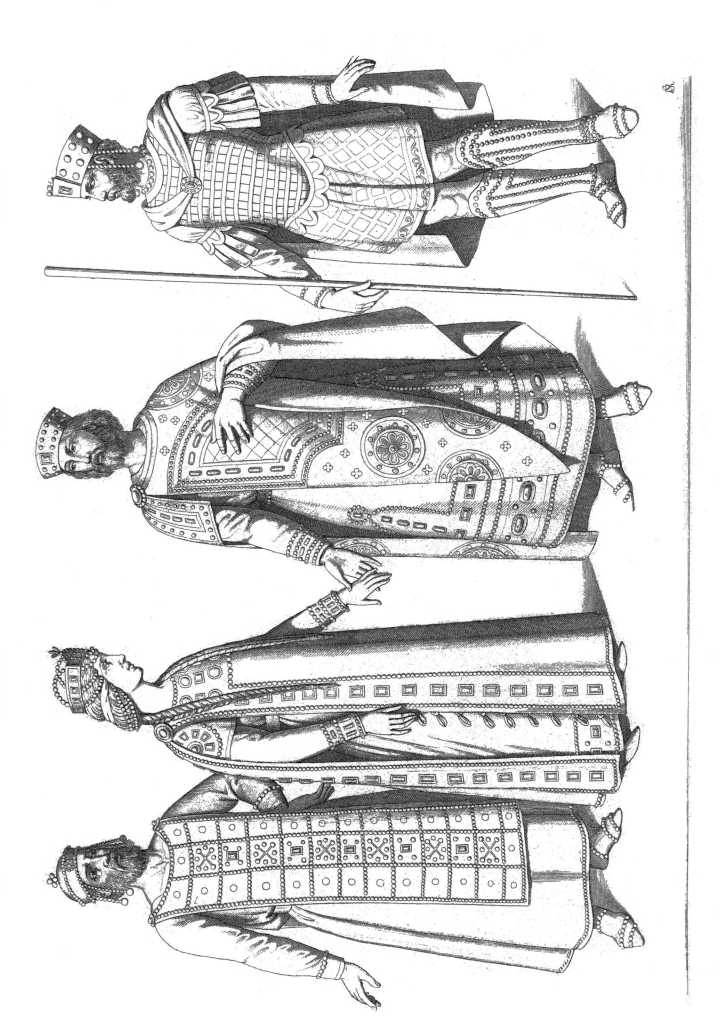

12   *Eastern Empire*
9th and 10th Centuries

1 Basil I, the Macedonian (867–886). 2 An empress. 3 An emperor. 4 Basil II, the
Younger (976–1025).

Sources: Mosaics and contemporary codices.

13 Eastern Empire
10th Century

1 Otto II, the Red, Emperor of Germany, son of Otto the Great and Adelaide of Burgundy, in the Garb of an Eastern Emperor. 2 The Empress Theophania, step-daughter of the Emperor Niceforo Foca and wife of Otto II. 3, 4, 5 Solomon, Zacharias, and Herod in Byzantine attire.

Sources: 2 Ivory intaglio in the Cluny Museum, Paris. 3–5 Codex in the Bibliothèque Nationale, Paris.

14 France

10th Century

1 St. Germain in ecclesiastical vestment. 2 A deacon. 3 A noble. 4 A monarch. 5 A monarch. 6 A gentlewoman.

Sources: 5 Miniature in the Bibliothèque Nationale, Paris. 6 Miniature in the Royal Library, Brussels.

15   *Germany*

10th Century

The Emperor Otto I (d. 973) and his wife Edith (d. 947). [*According to tradition the 19 pellets enclosed in the orb that the Emperor holds in his right hand represent the weight of gold he offered for the construction of the Cathedral of Magdeburg. The Empress holds the Gospel in her right hand, as was usual when depicting an empress on a throne.*]

Source: Statues in the Magdeburg Cathedral.

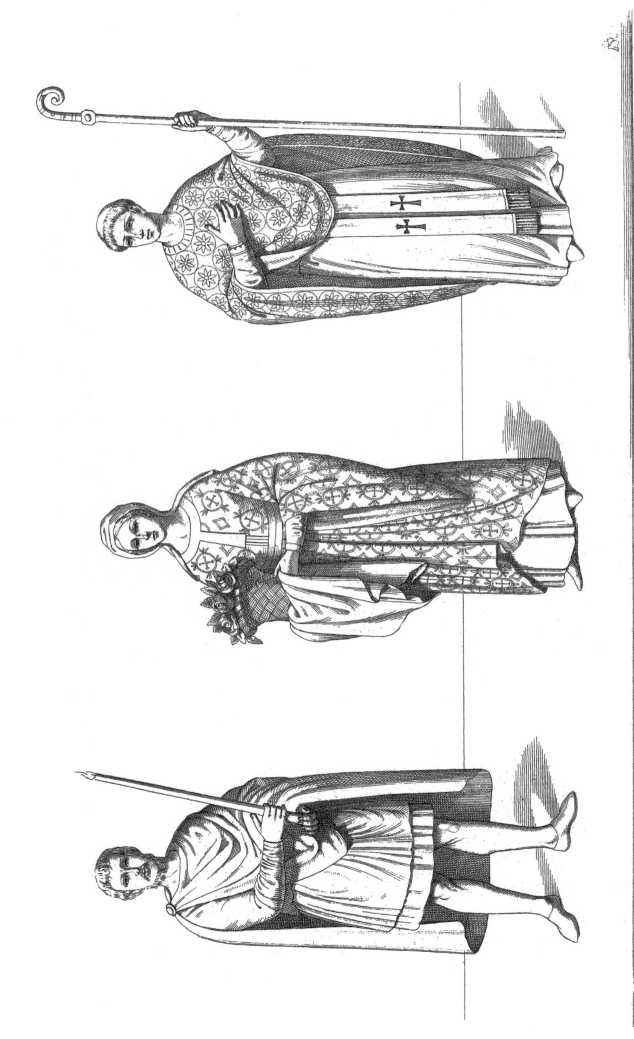

16   *Italy*

11th Century

Beno of Rapizia (d. 1080), Domma Maria, and St. Clement.

Source: Fresco in the Church of St. Clement, Rome.

17   *Eastern Empire*
11th Century

Military dress of the Byzantine court.

Sources: Miniatures representing St. Leontius, St. James the Persian, St. Mercury, and St. George, at the Louvre, Paris.

18 *France*

11th Century

1 A gentleman. 2 St. Radegonda, wife of Clothario I, in 11th-century costume. 3 A queen. 4 A knight. 5 An archer. 6 A hunter. 7 A peasant.

Sources: Codices in the Library of Düsseldorf and Trinity College, Cambridge.

19   *Germany*

11th Century

1 Bishop with a "pontifical tiara." 2 Priest in dalmatic.

Sources: 1 Contemporary codex in the Library of the University of Leipzig. [*The miniature from which the figure was taken represents Pope Gregory being inspired by the Holy Spirit.*]
2 11th-century codex in the Library of Stuttgart.

20   *Germany*
11th Century

1 Henry II, the Saint, King of Germany and Emperor of the West (d. 1024). 2 Rudolph of Swabia, son of Count Kuno of Rheinfelden (d. 1080). 3 Witikind, Saxon hero.

Sources: 1 Missal in the Library of Munich. 2 Funerary monument in the Cathedral of Merseberg. 3 Funerary monument in the Church of St. Denis, Angers.

21 *Anglo-Saxons*
11th Century

1, 2 Knights. 3 Feminine dress. 4, 5 Knights. 6 A soldier armed with shield. 7 An official of the Court. 8 King Harold II. 9 An official of the Court. 10 The Archbishop of Canterbury.

Sources: Ancient Saxon codices and the "Bayeux Tapestry."

22   *Anglo-Normans*

11th Century

1 Warrior of the time of Henry I. [*The warrior has a pointed helmet indented in front, with a fixed nasal in the Anglo-Saxon manner.*] 2 Richard Fitzhugh, Constable of Chester and standard-bearer of England. [*The standard-bearer leans upon the English standard, on which are depicted "leos-pardes," that is, lions passant with heads held majestically and tails curled backward.*]

Sources: 1 Ancient manuscript codex. 2 Richard Fitzhugh's seal. Shaw.

23   *Anglo-Saxons and Anglo-Danes*

11th Century

1, 2, 3 Warriors at the time of the Danish conquest. 4 A priest. 5, 6 Queen Aelgifu and King Canute of England and Denmark. 7, 8 Monks. 9 A shepherd. 10 Wulfstan, Bishop of York.

Sources: 1–3 Ancient Saxon reliquary. 4 Old ivory sculpture in the Würzburg Library. 9 Old codex in the Cottonian Library, British Museum. 10 Old codex in the Monastery of St. Augustine, Canterbury. Strutt.

24   *England*

11th and 12th Centuries

1 William the Conqueror. 2, 3, 4 Anglo-Norman nobles. 5, 6 Anglo-Norman citizens. 7, 8, 9 Anglo-Norman citizens in traveling clothes. 10, 11, 12 Peasants. 13 A Welsh knight.

Sources: Old codices in the Library of Rouen and from Corpus Christi College, Oxford.

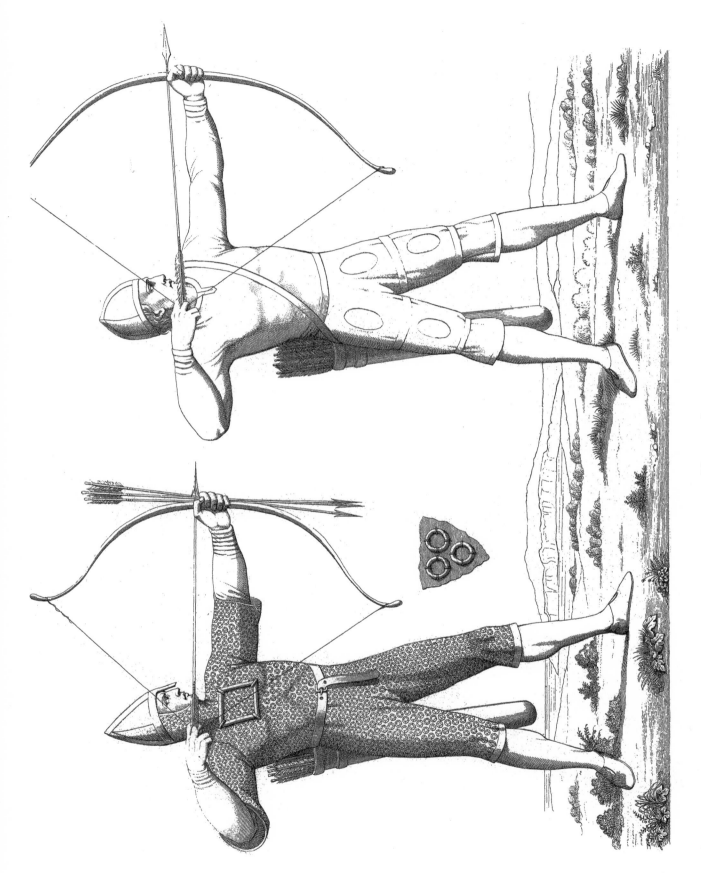

25 *Normandy*

11th Century

Archers

Sources: The "Bayeux Tapestry" preserved in the Bayeux Municipal Hall.

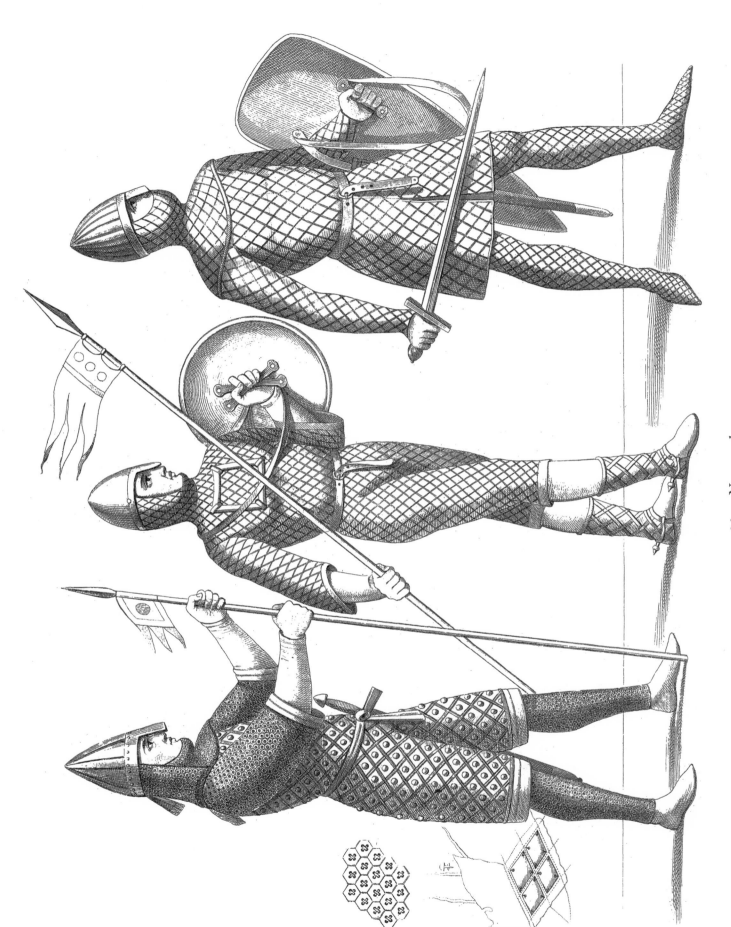

26 *Normandy*
11th Century

Knights, armor, composed of rings and small, rhombus-shaped plates, sewed onto a fabric suit.

Sources: The "Bayeux Tapestry"; Old codex in the British Museum; Meyrick.

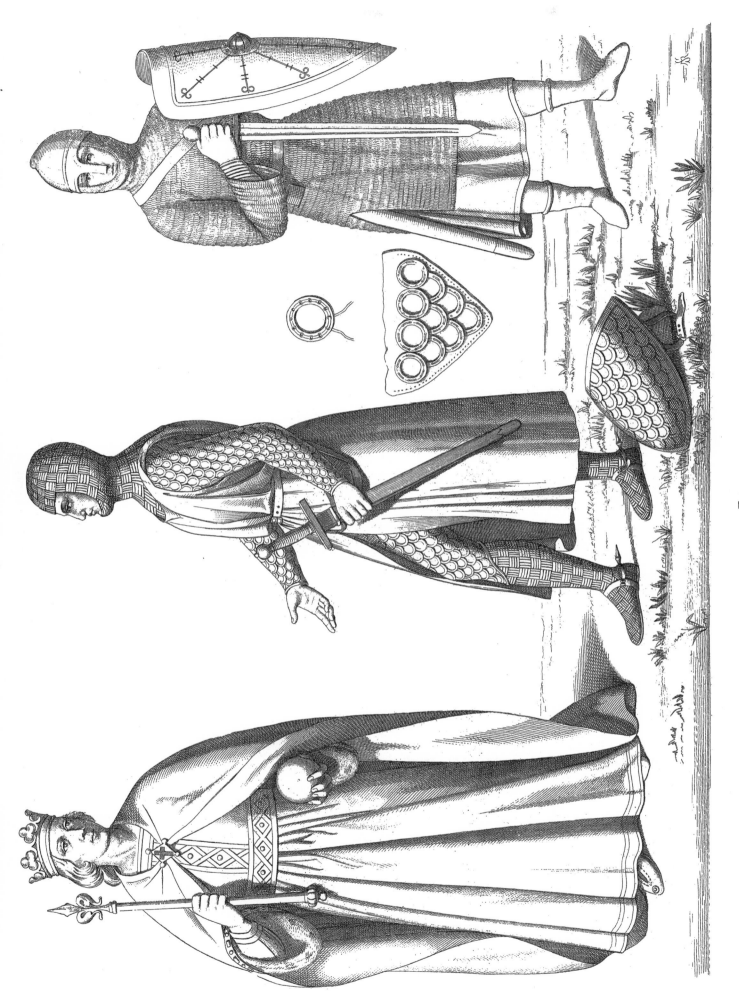

27 *France*

12th Century

1 A king. 2 Knight, with armor made of iron rings sewed on a resistant fabric and overlapping half way. 3 A knight, wearing a coat and coif of mail all of one piece.

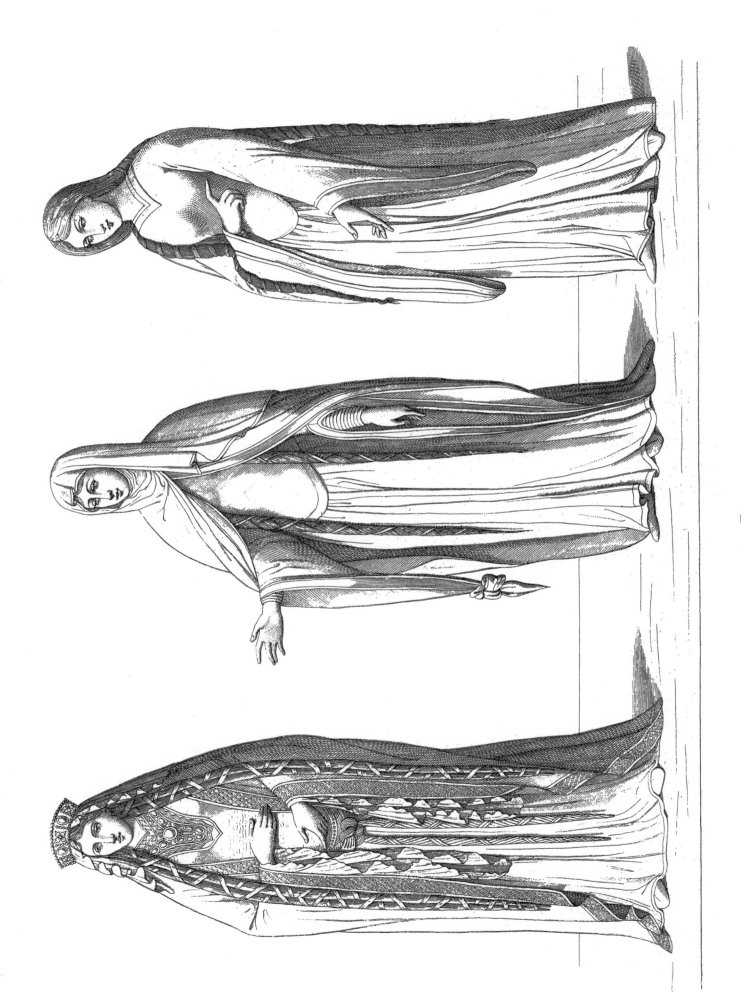

28   France

12th Century

1 Queen Clotilde, wife of King Clovis I. 2, 3 Norman ladies.

Sources: 1 Sculpture in St. Denis Cathedral. 2, 3 Funerary monuments shown in Montfaucon.

29   *France*
12th Century

1 An archbishop. 2 A deacon. 3 A priest.

Sources: Sculptures on the doors of the Cathedral of Chartres; Shaw.

30   *France*

12th Century

1 Constance of Castile, second wife of Louis VII (d. 1160). 2 Agnes of Baudemont, Lady of Braine, third wife of Robert of France, Count of Dreux. 3 Agnes of Baudemont.

Sources: 1 Funerary monument in the Church of Barbeaux. 2 A seal. 3 Her tomb in the choir of the Church of St. Ives of Braine, in the Abbey of Premontrez.

31 *France*
12th Century

1 A monarch, wearing a tunic embroidered in fleur-de-lis. 2 Geoffrey Plantagenet,
Count of Anjou and Maine. 3 Louis VII, the Younger (d. 1180).

Sources: 1 Miniature in a codex in the British Museum. 2 Enamel in the Museum of Mans.
3 Funerary monument in the Church of Barbeaux.

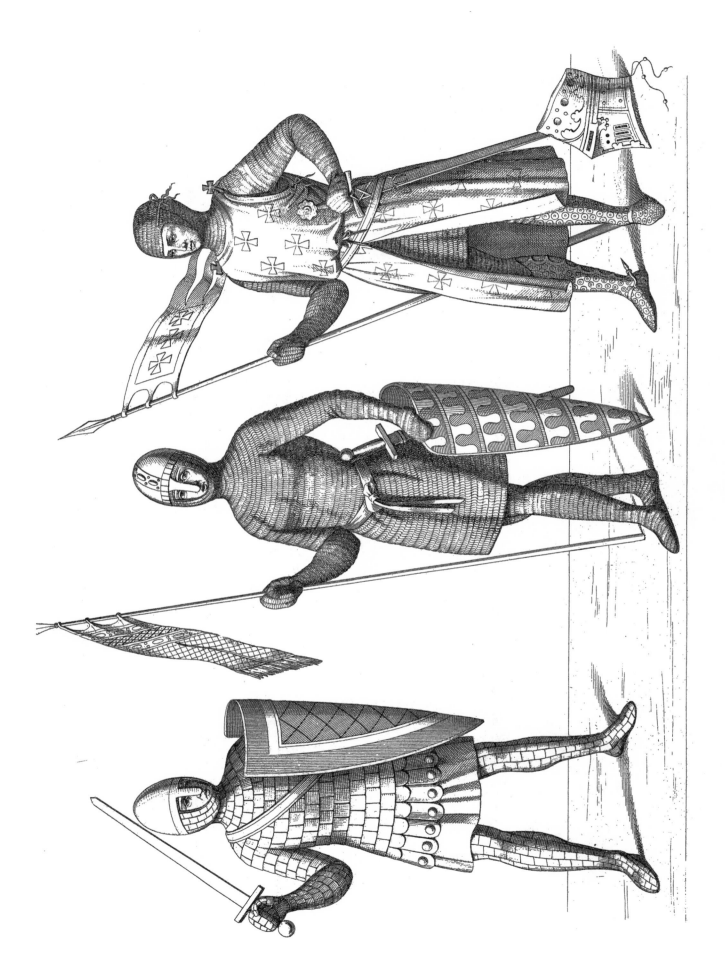

32 *Germany*
12th Century

Armor, end of the 12th century. [*The first figure wears "scale" armor, probably of leather; the third, complete mail covered with a surcoat and leather shin-guards, decorated with metal studs.*]

Sources: Hefner-Alteneck (1860 and 1879).

33　　*Germany and France*
12th Century

1 Gentlewoman of the middle of the 12th century. 2 Armor of mail. 3 Bishop Ulger (d. 1149).

Sources:　1 Miniature in a contemporary codex at the Convent of the Benedictines, Salzburg. 2 Miniature published by Hefner-Alteneck. 3 Enameled plate on Bishop Ulger's funerary monument, in the Church of St. Maurice, Angers. Hefner-Alteneck (1879).

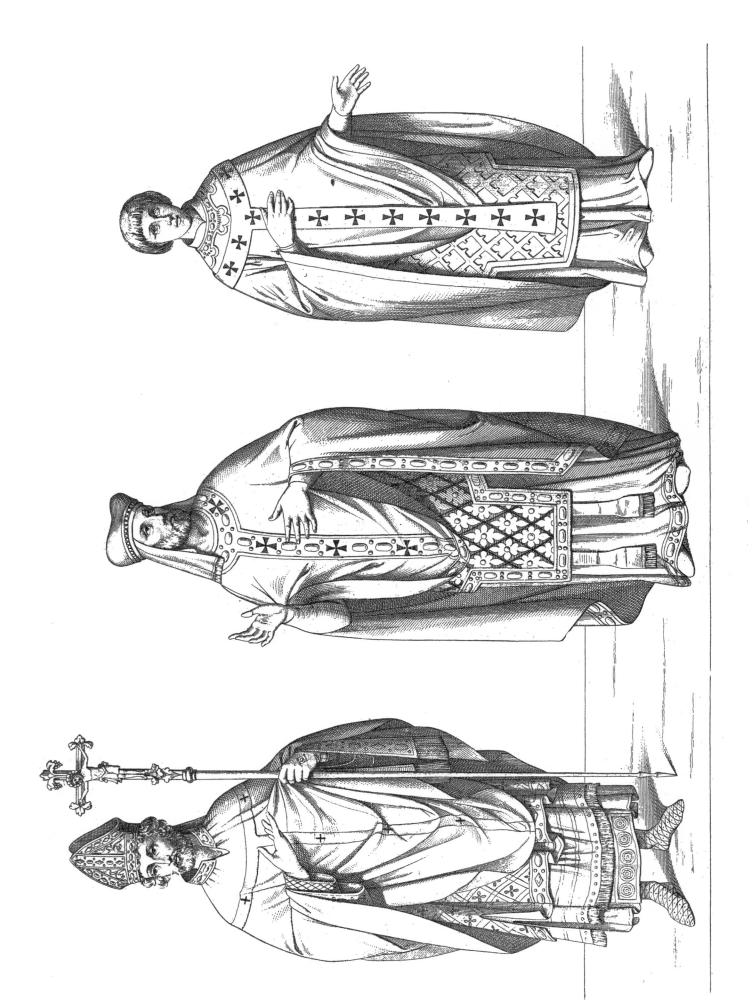

34   Anglo-Normans

12th Century

1 An archbishop in pontifical dress. 2, 3 A bishop and plate.

Sources: Codex of the end of the 12th century; old Psalter in the British Museum; Shaw.

35   *Scotland*

12th Century

1 Alexander I, King of Scotland. 2 David, Count Huntingdon, later King David of Scotland.

Sources: The seals of Alexander I and David; Meyrick.

36   *Normandy*

12th Century

1 William the Conqueror. 2 Men at Arms.

Sources: 1 William the Conqueror's knightly seal. 2 The "Bayeux Tapestry."

37 *Italy, Germany, France*

13th Century

1 Conrad on Thuringia (d. 1241) in the regalia of the Knights of the Teutonic Order (white cloak with black cross on the left shoulder). 2 John of Dreux (*fl.* 1275) a Knight Templar (white cloak with red cross on the left shoulder). 3 Knight of the Knights Hospitalers of St. John of Jerusalem (black cloak with white cross on the left shoulder).

Sources: 1 Tombstone in the Church of St. Elizabeth, Marburg. 2 Tombstone in the Church of St. Ives of Braine, near Soissons. 3 Bar.

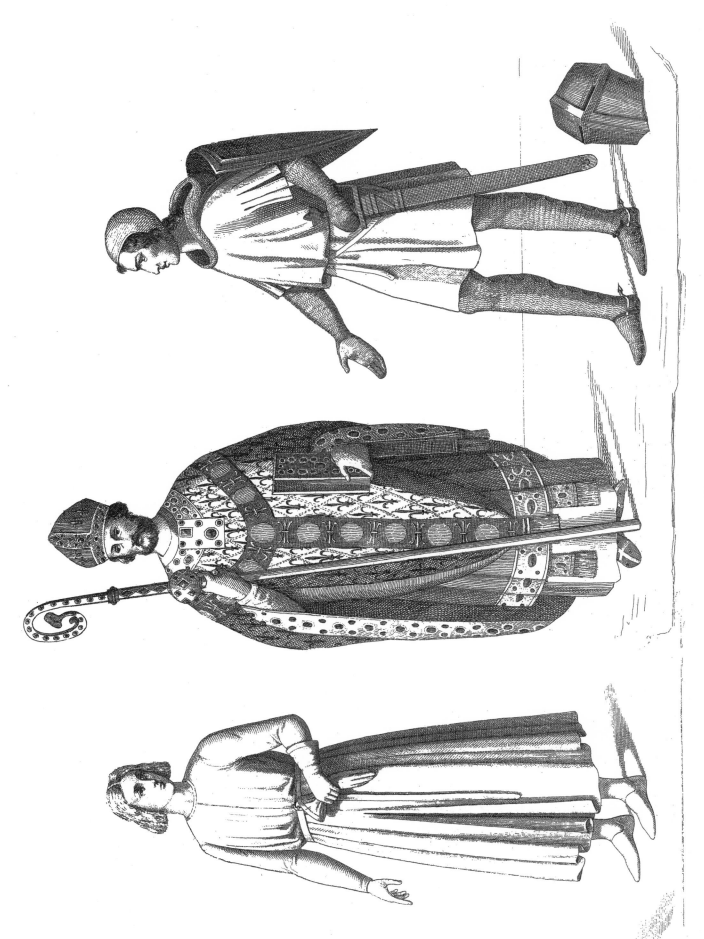

38 *France*

13th Century

1 Theobald of Sancerre. 2 Philip of Drew, Bishop of Beauvais (ca. 1227). 3 Knight of the time of King Louis, the "saint."

Sources: 1 Tombstone in the Chapter-house of the Abbey of Barbeaux. 3 Miniature published in Willemin.

39   *France*

13th Century

Knights and squires.

Sources: Paintings in the Castle of St. Floret, Alverne.

13 Century

1 Peter of Dreux, called "Mauclerc," Duke of Brittany and Count of Richemont. [*The
arms of the Duke are repeated on the surcoat, the shield, the ailettes, and on his
standard.*] 2 William of Harcourt, master chef of France. 3 Robert of Suzane (d. 1260),
fencing master.

Sources: 1 Window in the Church of Our Lady of Chartres. 2 Window in the Cathedral of Evreux.
3 Tombstone in the Abbey of Mont St. Quentin.

41   *France and England*

13th Century

Knights' armor and horse trappings. [*The first knight is clad in full mail with leg armor of boiled leather, rather than plate.*]

Sources: 1 The tomb of Sir Aimery of William Bernardi, Bailiff of Narbonne, who fell at Campaldino (1289), in the cloister of St. Annunziata, Florence. 2 Mural in Hewitt's Palace, England.

42 *Germany*
13th Century

1, 2 Men at arms wearing complete mail reinforced with metal plates. 3, 4 Count Ernest von Gleichen and his wife.

Source: 3, 4 Funerary monument at the Cathedral of Erfurt.

43   *Germany*

13th Century

1 Knights' armor. [*The strip of cloth attached to the last knight's helmet served in the beginning only to protect the head and shoulders from the sun; later this sendal became an essential part of the crest, as the mantlings called "lambrequins," and bore the same colors as the coat of arms.*] 2 Walther von Klingen in a tourney. [*Walther von Klingen, knight and troubador (d. ca. 1298), had two silver war axes on his crest. The horse's caparison is of the type used until the 16th century.*]

Sources: Miniature in a "machsor" (Hebrew prayer book). 2 Miniature of the facsimile of the Manesse Codex in the Bibliothèque Nationale, Paris.

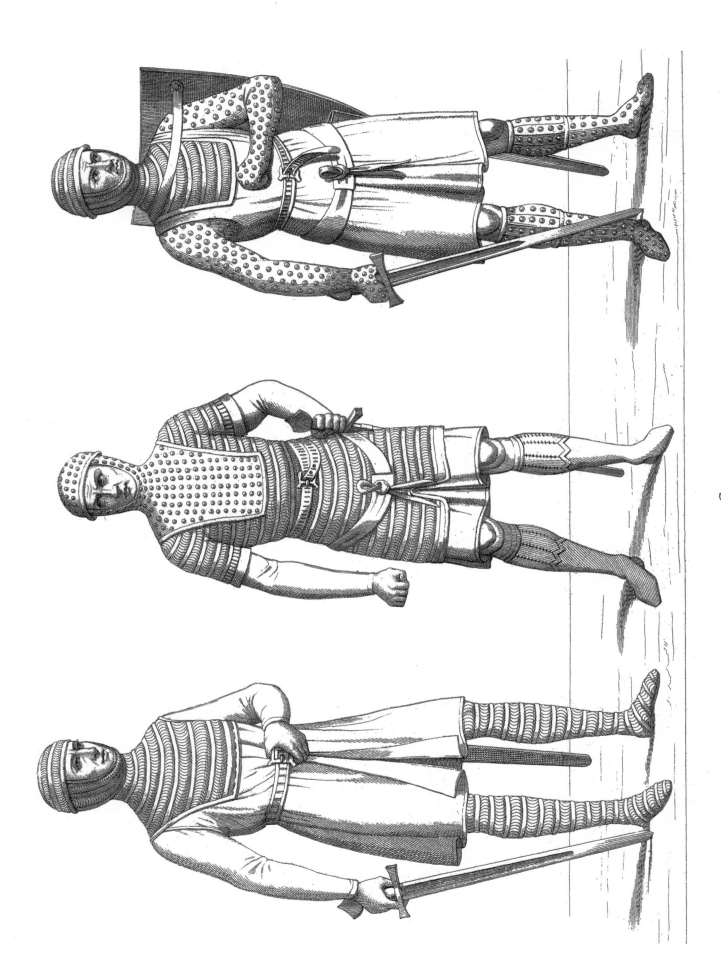

44 *Germany*
13th Century

Men at arms. [The coats of mail are intermeshed with leather thongs, according to the usage of the end of the 13th century, or with sections of iron plate covered with fabric or leather fastened with metal rivets.]

Source: Meyrick.

45   *England*
13th Century (end)

Knights' armor.

Sources: 1 The funerary monument of Sir Robert of Shurland, in the Church of Minster, Kent.
2 The funerary monument of William of Valence, Count of Pembroke, Westminster
Abbey. 3 The funerary monument of Sir John Laverik, Knight of Jerusalem, in the Church
of Ash, Kent.

46   *England*

13th Century (end)

Knights jousting.

Sources: Contemporary miniatures; Shaw.

47 *England*

13th Century (end)

1 Elenore, wife of Edward I (d. 1290). 2 Lady holding a child. 3 The Countess of Lancaster (d. 1269).

Sources: Funerary monuments.

48 *England*
13th Century

1 William Longuespée, Count of Salisbury (d. 1224). 2 Knight wearing surcoat. 3 Knight.
Sources: 2 Tomb in Norton, Durham. 3 Funerary monument in the Church of Ashby, Sandwich.

49   *Italy*
14th Century

1 Armor of the first half of the 14th century: Sir Thomas Buldanus (d. 1335). 2 Knight. 3 Knight.

Sources: 1 Tomb in the Church of St. Dominick Maggiore, Naples. 2 Tomb in the Church of St. Dominick Maggiore, Naples. 3 Sculpture in the Church of St. Eustorgio, Milan.

50   *Italy*

14th Century

Knights' armor.

Source: The funerary monument of A. Malaspina (d. 1637) in Fosdinovo.

51   *Italy*

14th Century

Dress and hairstyles of a girl and a youth of the nobility.

Source: An Italian manuscript of 1300, "The Romance of the Holy Grail," in the Bibliothèque Nationale, Paris.

52   *Eastern Empire*

14th Century

Dress and fashion at the Court of Byzantium.

Source: Mosaics of the Baptistry of St. Mark's, Venice. [*The warriors' armor, however, seems to belong to an earlier period than the designated 14th century.*]

53   *Eastern Empire*
      14th Century

Dress and fashion at the Court of Byzantium.

Source: Mosaics of the Baptistry of St. Mark's, Venice. [*The warriors' armor, however, seems to belong to an earlier period than the designated 14th century.*]

54   *Germany*

14th Century

1 Günther von Schwartzburg, King of the Romans (d. 1349). 2 Knight from the second half of the 14th century. 3 Hartman von Kroneberg (d. 1372). 4 Ulrich Landschader ("Scourge of the Land", d. 1369). [*Ulrich was a crusader in 1344. After killing a Saracen chief at the siege of Smyrna, he carried his effigy as a crest.*]

Sources: 1 Tomb in the Cathedral of Frankfort on Main. 2 Wooden sculpture in the choir of the Cathedral of Bamberg. 3 Tomb in the old chapel of the Castle of Kroneberg. 4 Tomb in the Church of Neckarsteinach, near Heidelberg.

55   *Germany*
14th Century

Knights of the second half of the 14th century.

Sources: The tombstones of Hartman von Kroneberg (d. 1372), and the funerary monument of
Konrad von Bickenback (d. 1393) in Roellfeld.

56 *Germany*

14th Century

Knights' armor.

Sources: The funerary monuments of Albrecht von Hohenlohe (d. 1319), Peter Kreglinger (d. 1319), and others.

57   *England*

14th Century

Dress and hairstyles of the nobility.

Sources: The sculptures on the tomb of Sir Roger of Kerdeston (d. 1337), in the Church of
Reepham, Norfolk. [*The figures represent the relatives of the deceased.*]

58   *England*

14th Century

1 Sir Oliver Ingham (d. 1344). 2 Sir Miles of Stapleton, with his wife (d. 1364). 3 Blansh-front (d. 1346).

Sources: Funerary monuments.

59   *England*
14th Century

1 Thomas Cheyne, Esq. (d. 1368). 2 John Grey, Esq. (d. 1390). 3 Sir John of St. Quintin (d. 1397). 4 (unknown). 5 Sir George Felbrigge (d. 1400).

Sources: Funerary monuments.

60   *England*

14th Century

Knight's armor and feminine dress.

Sources: 1, 2 The funerary monument of the Northwood family, in the Church of Minster, on the Island of Sheppy. 3 The funerary monument of a gentlewoman of the Nevill of Raby family, in the Church of Staindrop, Durham.

61   *England*

14th Century

Knights' armor.

Sources: Contemporary funerary monuments.

62   England

14th Century

Knights' armor.

Sources: The tombs of Edward, the Black Prince (d. 1376), in the Cathedral of Canterbury, and of
Sir Thomas Cawne, in the Church of Ingham, Kent.

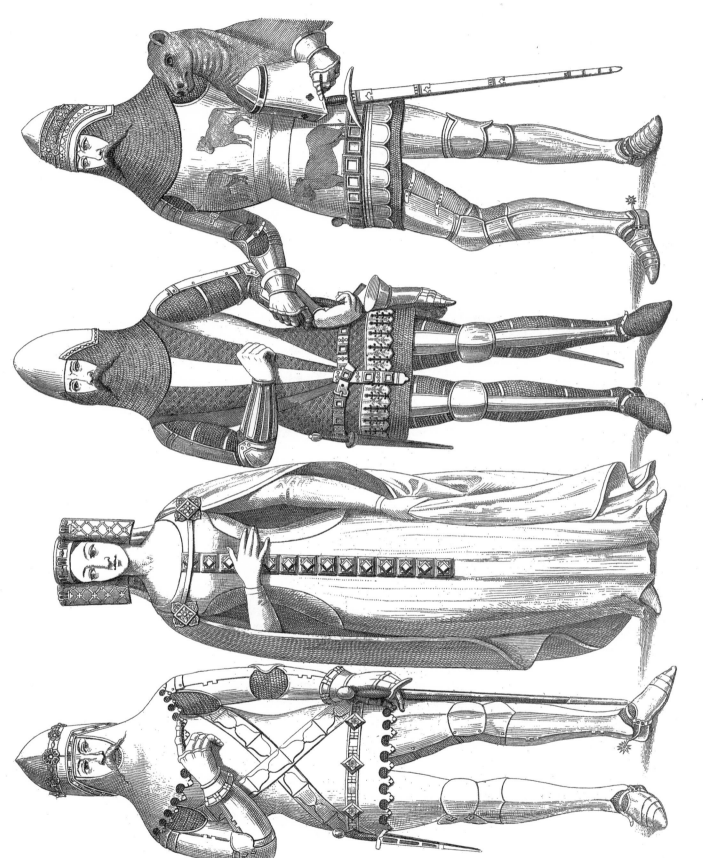

63 *England*

14th Century

Knights' armor and feminine dress.

Sources: 1, 2 The tomb of Sir Arthur Basset and his wife, Eleanor, at Atherington. 3 The tomb of Sir Guy Brian, in Tewkesbury Abbey. 4 The sepulchre of Sir Hugh Calvely in the Church of Bunbury, Cheshire.

64 *Spain*
14th Century

Dress and armor in vogue at the end of the 14th century.

Source: Hottenroth.

65   *Spain*
14th Century (end)
Moorish arms and dress.

Source: Hottenroth.

66   *Italy*

15th Century

Armor and military styles.

Source: The frescoes by Luca Signorelli at Monteoliveto Maggiore, Siena.

67   *Italy*

15th Century

Armor and military Styles.

Source: The frescoes by Luca Signorelli at Monteoliveto Maggiore, Siena.

68   Italy

15th Century

Armor of the second half of the 15th century.

Sources: 1 St. Alexander, by Bernardo Zenale (Pinacoteca di Brera). 2 Francesco Gonzaga, by Andrea Mantegna (Louvre). 3 St. Eustace, by Lazzaro Bastiani (Accademia, Venice). 4 Federico d'Urbino, by Pier della Francesca (Pinacoteca di Brera).

69   Italy

15th Century

Francesco Sforza and his wife.

Source: Painting by Giulio Campi in the Church of St. Sigismondo, Cremona.

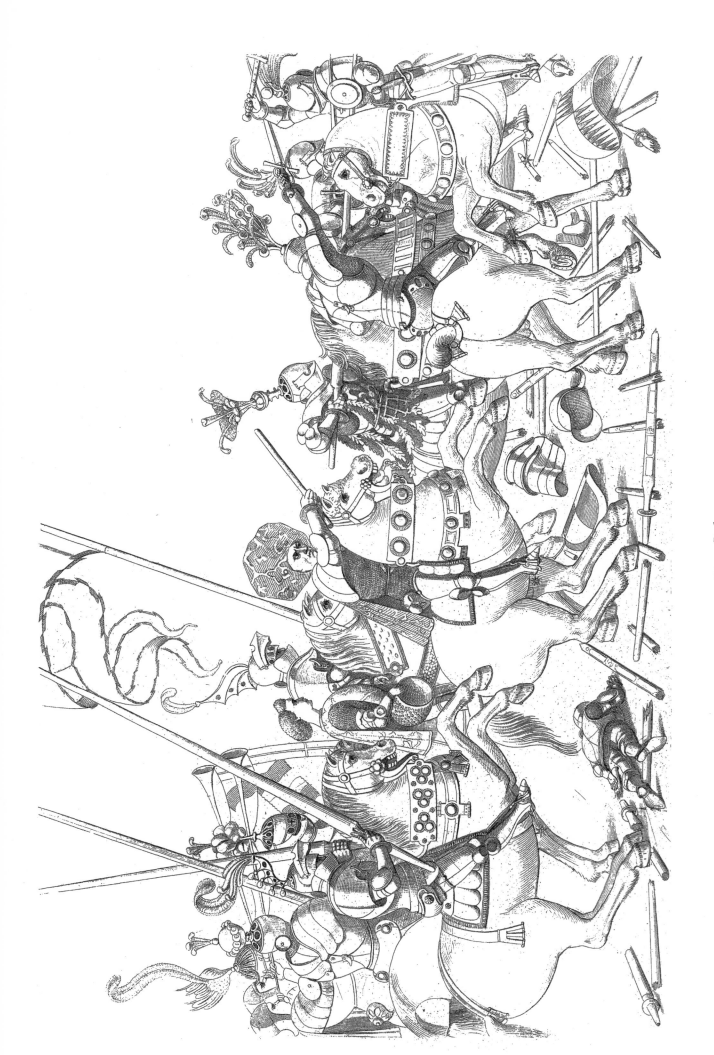

70   *Italy*

15th Century

Armor of the second half of the 15th century. [The knights' heads are protected by
the "close helmet," of Italian origin ("armets"), which, toward the middle of the
century, displaced the old sallets which always carried a bevor that covered the lower
part of the face.]

Source: The "Battle of St. Egidio," by Paolo Uccello.

71   *Italy*

15th Century

Field armor of various styles.

Source: The frescoes of Pier della Francesca, in the Church of St. Francis at Assisi.

15th Century

1 Antonio Ridi, Paduan noble, general in charge of the Church militia in the pontificate of Niccolo V. 2 Giordano Orsini. 3, 4 Count Giovanni Bentivoglio. 5 A knight. 6 Paolo Savelli. 7 St. George.

Sources: 1 The equestrian portrait in the Church of St. Francesca Romana, Rome. 2 The equestrian portrait in the Church of Monte Rotondo. 3 Old drawing. 4 Monument in the Church of St. Giacomo Maggiore, Bologna. 5 Painting by Vanni, Academy of Fine Arts, Siena. 6 Funerary monument in the Church of the Frari, Venice. 7 Miniature attributed to Memling in the Grimani Breviary.

73   *Italy*

15th Century (second half)

1 St. George in armor of the end of the 15th century. [*The saintly knight has a plumed hat over his skull cap.*] 2 St. George in the armor of the end of the 15th century. [*The unusual form of the shoulder-guards and the large straw hat, a Tuscan style, should be noted.*] 3 St. Michael in armor of the end of the 15th century. 4 St. Sebastian in archer's armor. 5 St. Michael in armor of the end of the 15th century.

Sources: 1 Painting by Amico Aspertino in the Pinacoteca of Lucca. 2 Painting by Pisanello in the National Gallery, London. 3 Painting by Perugino in the National Gallery, London. 4 Miniature in the Grimani Breviary. 5 Painting by Francesco Botticini in the Gallery of the Accademia, Florence.

74   *Italy*
15th Century

Venetian dress and styles of the second half of the 15th century.

Source: Painting by Vittore Carpaccio in the Church of S. Giorgio degli Schiavoni, Venice.

75   *Italy*
15th Century

Venetian dress. [Some of the personages wear attire with the insignia of rank of the
"Compagnia della Calza," a famous band of gay young gentlemen.]

Sources: The paintings of Vittore Carpaccio in the Gallery of the Accademia, Venice.

76   *Italy*
15th Century

Venetian dress of the end of the 15th century.

Source: The "History of St. Ursula," by Vittore Carpaccio in the Gallery of the Accademia, Venice.

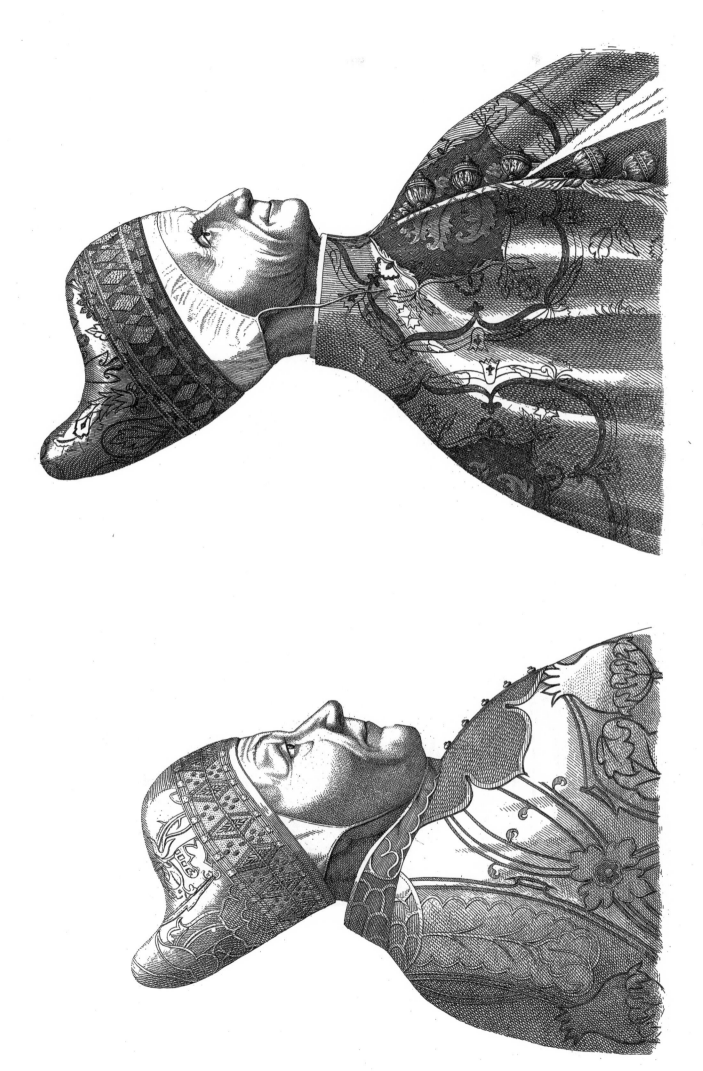

77   *Italy*

15th Century

1 Doge Francesco Foscari (1423–1457). 2 Doge Leonardo Loredano (1431–1521).

Sources: 1 Portrait in the Museo Civico, Venice. 2 Painting of the school of Gentile Bellini, in the Museo Civico, Venice.

78 *Italy*

15th Century

Masculine hairstyle.

Source: The "Portrait of an Unknown Man," by Ambrogio da Predis, in the Uffizi Gallery, Florence.

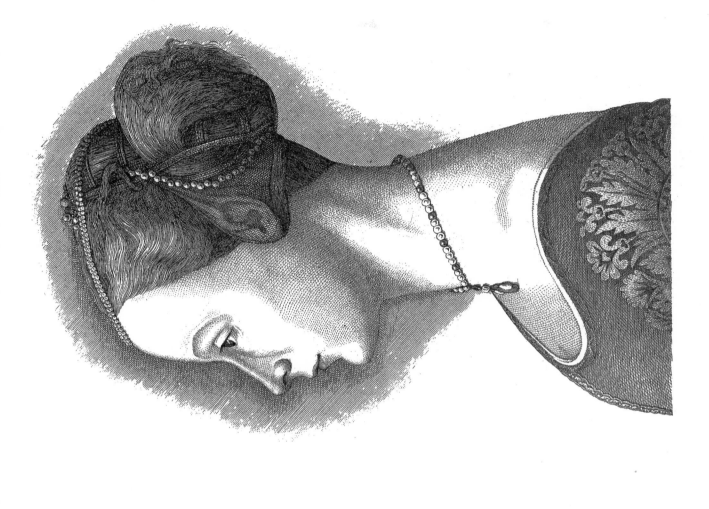

79 *Italy*
15th Century

1 Battista di B. Sforza, Duchess of Urbino, wife of Federigo di Montefeltro. 2 An Italian gentlewoman.

Sources: 1 Painting by Pier della Francesca, in the Uffizi Gallery, Florence. 2 15th-century portrait, attributed to A. Pollaiuolo, in the Poldi-Pezzoli Museum, Milan.

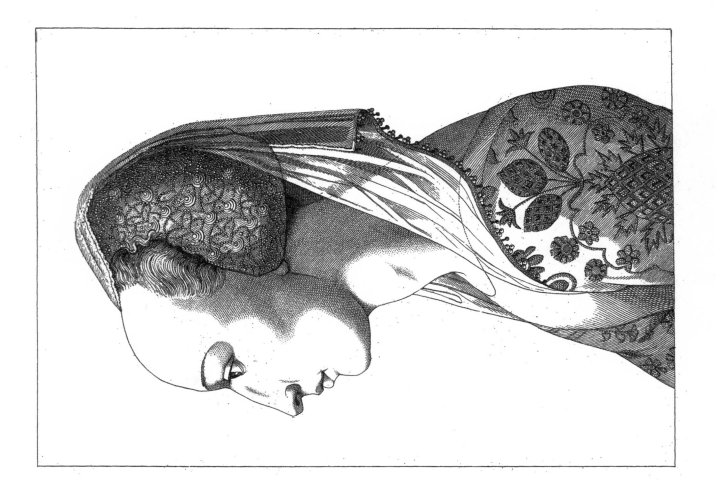

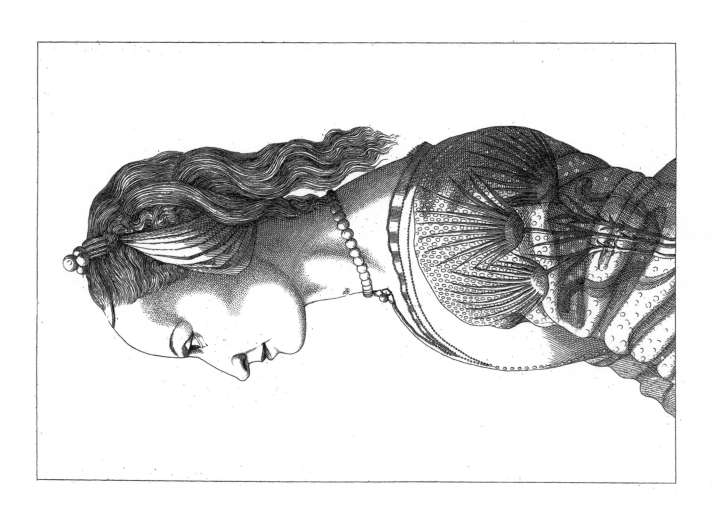

80   *Italy*

15th Century

1 Portrait (unknown). 2 Isotta da Rimini (?).

Sources: 1 Painting by Pier della Francesca, in the National Gallery, London. 2 Painting of the Umbrian School.

81   *Italy*
15th Century

Feminine hairstyles.

Sources: 1 Painting by Sandro Botticelli, in the Städelsches Museum, Frankfort. 2 Painting by Bartolommeo Veneto (formerly attributed to Dürer), in the Städelsches Museum, Frankfort.

15th Century

Feminine hairstyles and dress.

Sources: Supposed portrait of Lucretia Borgia and a painting by Bernardino de' Conti.

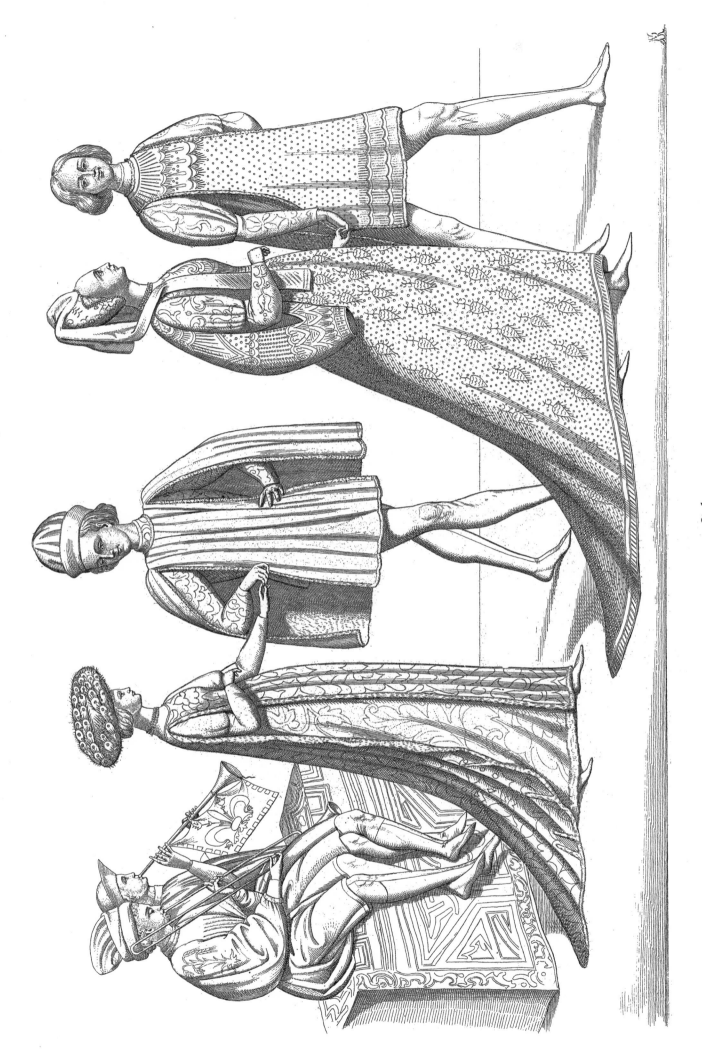

83   *Italy*

15th Century

Florentine dress of the first half of the 15th century.

Source: Painting on the front panel of a marriage chest, representing the Adimari-Ricasoli nuptials, by the mid-15th century Master of Fucecchio, in the Gallery of the Accademia, Florence.

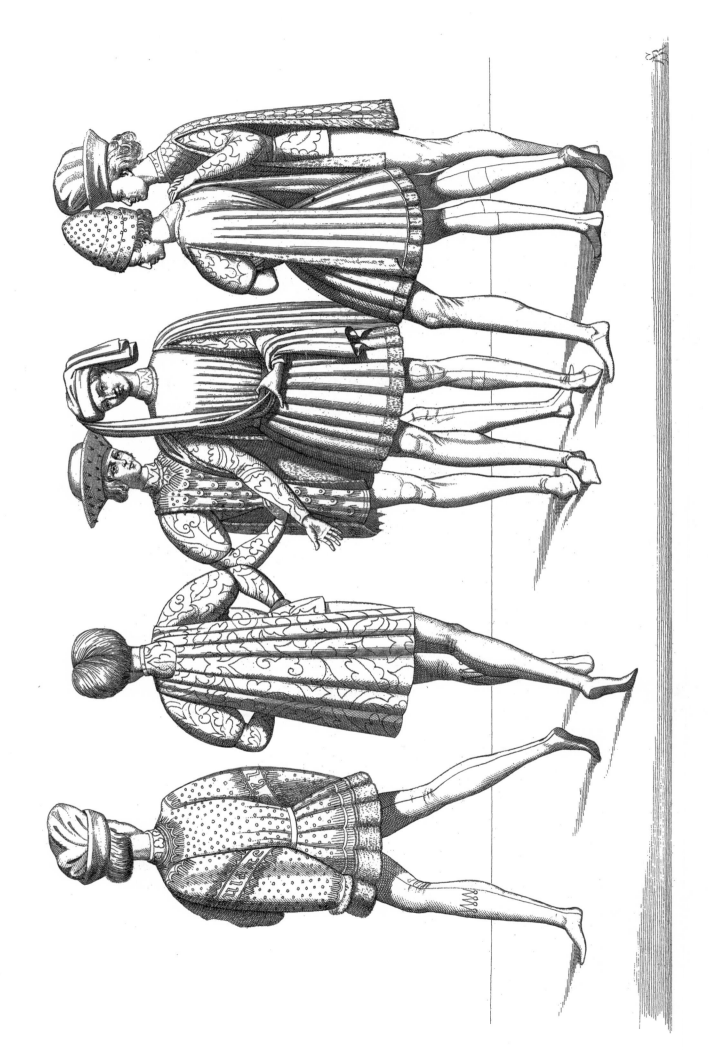

84　　*Italy*
15th Century

Florentine dress of the first half of the 15th century.

Source: Painting on the front panel of a marriage chest, representing the Adimari-Ricasoli nuptials, in the Gallery of the Accademia, Florence.

85 *Italy*

15th Century

A gentleman on horseback, in ceremonial dress.

Source: The frescoes by Benozzo Gozzoli, in the Chapel of the Riccardi Palace, Florence.

86 *Italy*

15th Century

Knights and pages.

Source: The "Journey of the Magi," by Benozzo Gozzoli, in the Chapel of the Riccardi Palace, Florence.

87   Italy

15th Century

Group of knights. [*In this group of knights—some of whom wear plate armor and others armor of boiled leather, called "à la Roman"—the very high crests made of papier-mâché, plumes, and cotton wool are noteworthy.*]

Source: The frescoes by Pier della Francesca, in the Church of St. Francis, Arezzo.

88 *Italy*

15th Century

Masculine hairstyles.

Source: The frescoes in the Castle of Manta (Saluzzo).

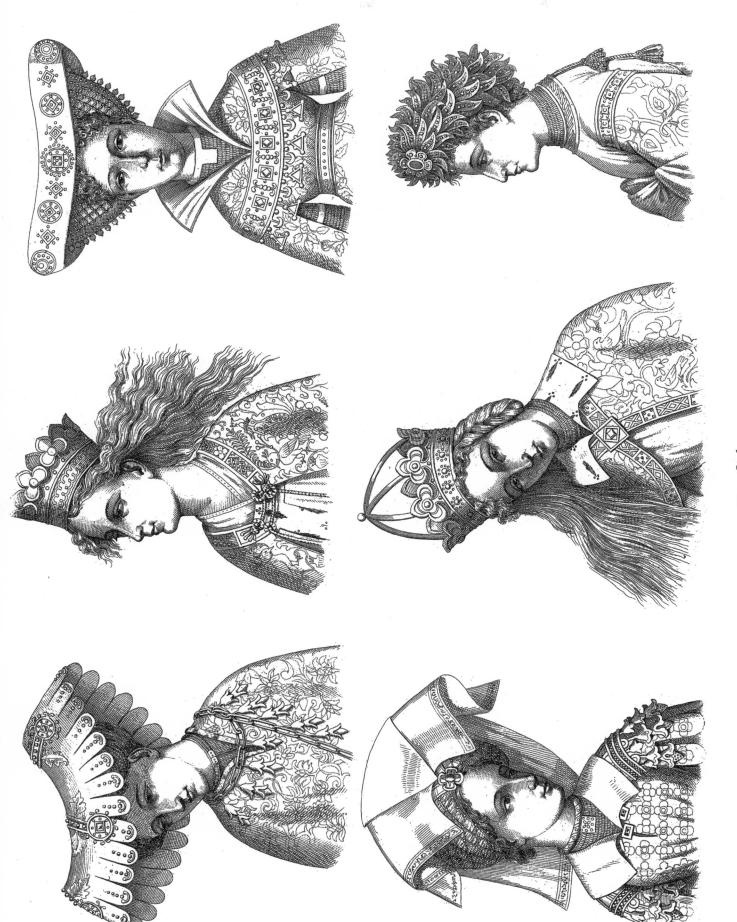

89   *Italy*
15th Century

Feminine hairstyles.

Source: The frescoes in the Castle of Manta (Saluzzo).

15th Century

1 Foot soldier of the second half of the 15th century. [*The soldier's head is protected by a sallet reinforced in the brow region, and he wears a cuirass decorated with ridges simulating the pleats of the doublet.*] 2 St. George. [*The Saint's armor is a magnificent example of the military outfit of the second half of the 15th century.*] 3 Man at arms. [*The soldier wears a mail hauberk, which is a cuirass of plate with tassets. His hose is richly embroidered and the greaves are without kneecaps, in the Italian manner.*]

Sources: 1 Painting by Vittore Carpaccio, in the Gallery of the Accademia, Venice. 2 Painting by Mantegna, in the Gallery of the Accademia, Venice. 3 Painting by Cima da Conegliano.

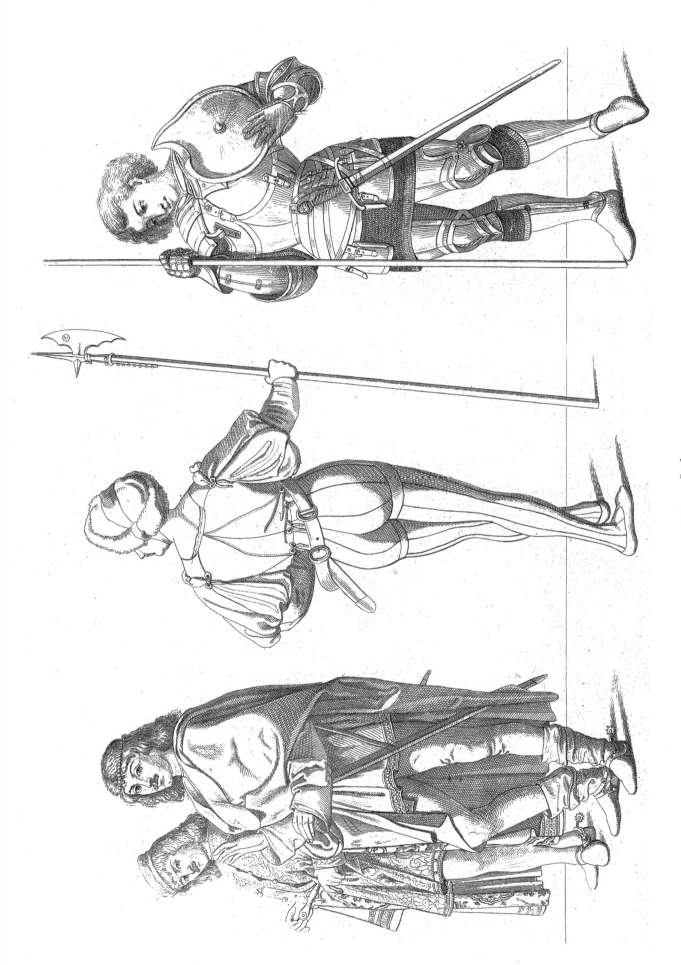

91   Italy
15th Century

1, 2 Knights. 3 Lombard foot soldier. 4 St. George. [*The armor is black, bordered in gold, a not too common practice at this time. The reinforcing plates of the shoulder defense is also not usual.*]

Sources: 1 Painting by Bartolommeo Montagna, in the Church of St. Nazzaro and St. Celso, Verona. 2 Painting by Andrea de Milano, in the Louvre, Paris. 3 Triptych by Michele Gambone, in the Gallery of the Accademia, Venice.

92　*Italy*
15th Century

1 Cristino Francesco I, son of Galeotto Bevilacqua, of the Barons Bevilacqua of Verona
(died Ferrara, 1468). 2 High official of the 15th century.

Sources:　Paintings in the Stibbert Museum.

93 *Italy*

15th Century

Group of men at arms. [*The varieties of armor are good examples of the military outfits of the end of the 15th century, and most all have kneecaps edged with a fringe of mail, an entirely Italian characteristic. The bearded soldier with the crowned head is wearing a brigandine, a kind of corselet made of small, overlapping iron plates attached to outer layers of fabric by rivets.*]

Source: Painting by Vittore Carpaccio, in the Gallery of the Accademia, Venice.

94   Italy

15th Century

Erasmo da Narni, called "Il Gattamelata." [*The armor of the military leader is in the style called "Roman." The spurs, exceptionally long, came into use towards the middle of the 15th century because of the new horse armor of plate. A celebrated example of the "Roman" armor is that of Charles V, preserved in Madrid. There is another example of this style of armor in the Royal Armory of Turin.*]

Source: Donatello's monument, Padua.

95 *Italy*

15th Century (end)

A captain with his squire. [*Noteworthy is the unusual style of the pauldrons and the very beautiful sallet with visor.*]

Source: Painting attributed to Paolo Morando Cavazzola, in the Uffizi Gallery, Florence.

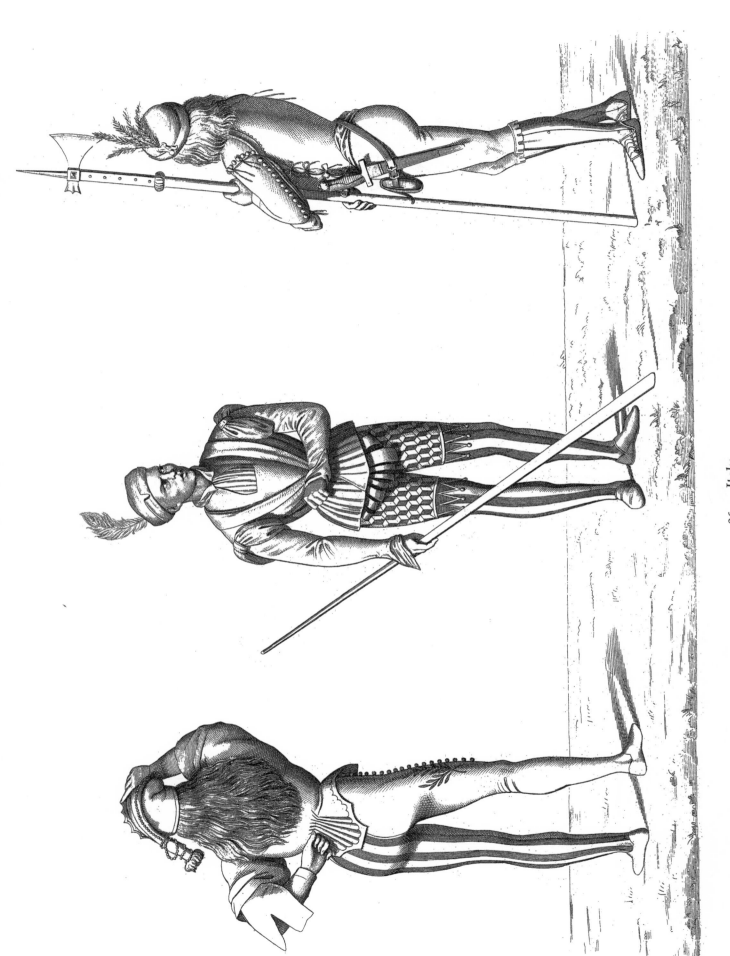

96   *Italy*

15th Century

1 Venetian youth of the "Campagnia della Calza." 2 Moorish gondolier. 3 Foot soldier armed with poleaxe.

Sources: Paintings by Vittore Carpaccio, 1 in the Accademia, Venice; 2 in the Uffizi, Florence.

97   *Italy*

15th Century

Ecclesiastical vestments of the end of the 15th century.

Source: The "Death of St. Girolamo," by Vittore Carpaccio, in the Church of S. Giorgio degli
Schiavoni, Venice.

98 *Italy*

15th Century

St. George slaying the dragon. [*The Saint wears the "Gothic" armor in general use in the 15th century, and which remained the unsurpassed model of armor because of its elegance. In addition, the armor presents an Italian characteristic of the 14th and 15th centuries: kneecap with mail edging falling down over the greave. The only examples of this extremely rare detail preserved are in the Stibbert Museum and the Wallace Collection in Hertford House.*]

Source: The painting by Vittore Carpaccio, in the Church of S. Giorgio degli Schiavoni, Venice.

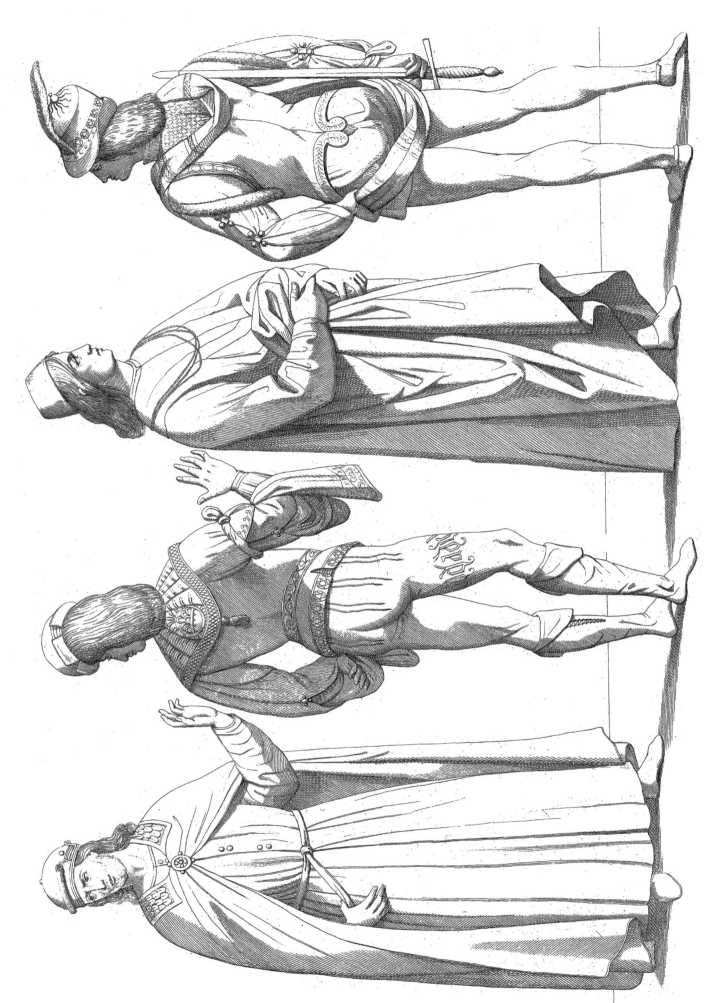

99   *Italy*

15th Century (end)

Masculine dress and hair-styles.

Sources: The frescoes by Cosimo Rosselli and Luca Signorelli, in the Sistine Chapel in the Vatican.

100 *Italy*

15th Century

Masculine dress and hairstyles.

Sources: The frescoes by Cosimo Rosselli and Luca Signorelli, in the Sistine Chapel in the Vatican.

101   *Italy*

15th Century

Tuscan dress of the mid-15th century.

Source: The frescoes by Benozzo Gozzoli, in the Church of St. Augustine, San Gimignano.

102   *Italy*

15th Century

Tuscan dress of the mid-15th century.

Source: The frescoes by Benozzo Gozzoli, in the Church of St. Augustine, San Gimignano.

103 *Italy*

15th Century

Generalissimo Bartolommeo Colleoni, by Andrea del Verrocchio. [*The general's armor and the horse's harness on this well-known monument are beautiful examples of the military style of the second half of the 15th century. Note the massive pauldrons which overlap at the back of the cuirass. Also worthy of attention is the movement of the horse, which paces in accordance with the best rules of the day, which demanded this gait for the palfrey, or show horse. This gait is found, in fact, in the equestrian portrait of Giovanni Acuto painted by Paolo Uccello in Santa Maria del Fiore, and on Gattamelata's horse done by Donatello.*]

104 *Italy*

15th Century

The Marquis Ludovico III Gonzaga with his family and Court.

Source: The frescoes by Andrea Mantegna, in the Castle of Mantua.

105   *Italy*

15th Century

Warhorse and Moorish squires.

Source: The "Triumph of St. George," by Vittore Carpaccio, in the Church of S. Giorgio degli Schiavoni, Venice.

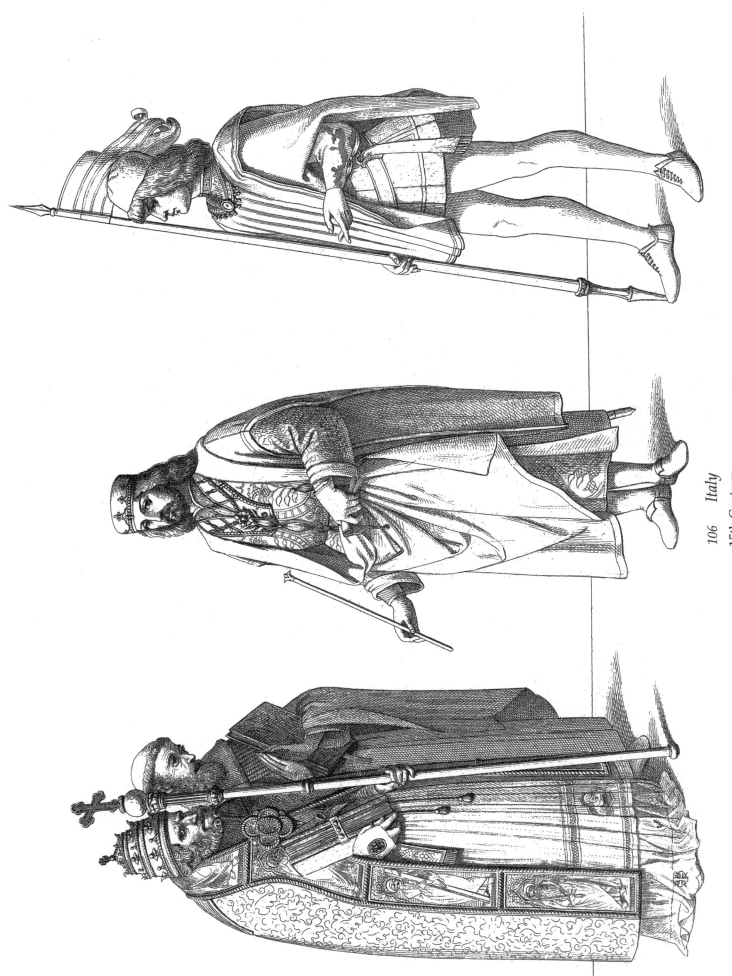

106   *Italy*

15th Century

1, 2 St. Peter dressed as Pope and St. Dominick as a monk. 3 Emperor Sigismund dressed as a Milanese nobleman. 4 San Gimignano dressed as a Venetian nobleman.

Sources: Triptych by Carlo Crivelli, in the Brera Gallery, Milan. 2 Painting by Bartolommeo Montagna, in the Brera Gallery. 4 Triptych by Carlo Crivelli.

107   *Italy*

15th Century

St. George in armor of the second half of the 15th century.

Source: The "Triumph of St. George," by Vittore Carpaccio, in the Church of S. Giorgio degli
Schiavoni, Venice.

108 Italy

15th Century

"Fluted" armor for man and horse, belonging to Cardinal Ascanio Maria Sforza Visconti.

Source: The Royal Armory, Turin.

109   Germany
15th Century (first half)

1 Ritter Kenebel von Katzenelbogen (d. 1401). 2 Count Johan von Werthein (d. 1401).
3 Ludwig von Kutten (d. 1414).

Sources: Funerary monuments.

110   *Germany*

15th Century

Armor and military styles.

Source: The polyptych by Stefan Lochner, in the Cathedral of Cologne.

111 *Germany*

15th Century

Feminine fashions.

Source: The polyptych by Stefan Lochner, in the Cathedral of Cologne.

112 *Germany*

15th Century

Complete plate armor of the second half of the 15th century. [*These suits of armor are two beautiful and rare examples of the perfection the art of the armorer attained in the 15th century. In both examples the head is protected with the sallet and the lower part of the face by the bevor. Later the closed helmet, or armet, of Italian origin, took the place of the sallet and the bevor.*]

Source: The Imperial Armory, St. Petersburg.

113 *Germany*

15th Century

Complete plate armor of the second half of the 15th century.

Source: The Imperial Armory, Vienna.

114   Germany

15th Century

Jousting and tournament armor and horse trappings.

Source: Contemporary prints illustrating jousts and tourneys in the time of Emperor Maximilian I

115 *Germany*

15th Century (end)

Jousting and tournament armor and horse trappings.

Source: Contemporary prints illustrating jousts and tourneys in the time of Emperor Maximilian I.

116 *Germany*
15th Century (end)

Jousting and tournament armor and horse trappings.

Source: Contemporary prints illustrating jousts and tourneys in the time of Emperor Maximilian I

117   *Germany*
15th Century (end)
A tourney.

Source: Hefner-Alteneck (1879).

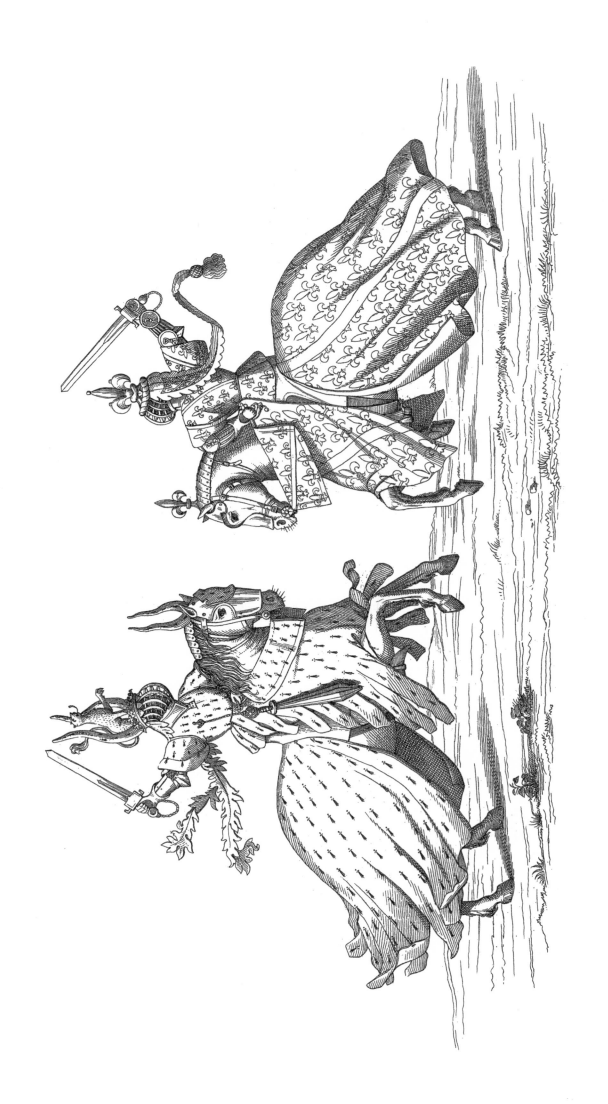

118   France

15th Century (second half)

Tourney between the Dukes of Brittany and Bourbon (1440).

Source: The "Book of Tourneys of King René (d'Anjou)."

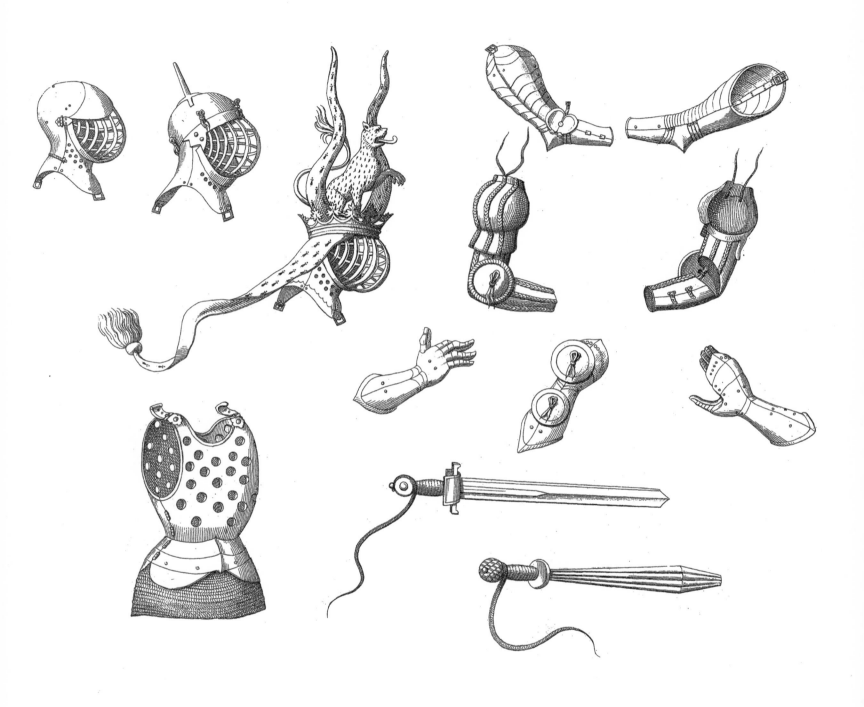

119　*France*

15th Century

Pieces of jousting armor. [*The iron basinet has a barred face guard and attached on top is the crest. The basinet was buckled to the breast- and back-plate by means of two straps. The cuirass is lightened by means of numerous perforations; under it the knight wore a cloth jerkin with padding under the shoulders and around the arms. The arm defenses and gauntlets were of plate, as in battle dress, or of boiled leather. The offensive weapons consisted of a blunted sword, that is, one without a point or whetted edge, or a wooden mace with a metal rondel in a grip area.*]

Source:　Viollet-le-Duc.

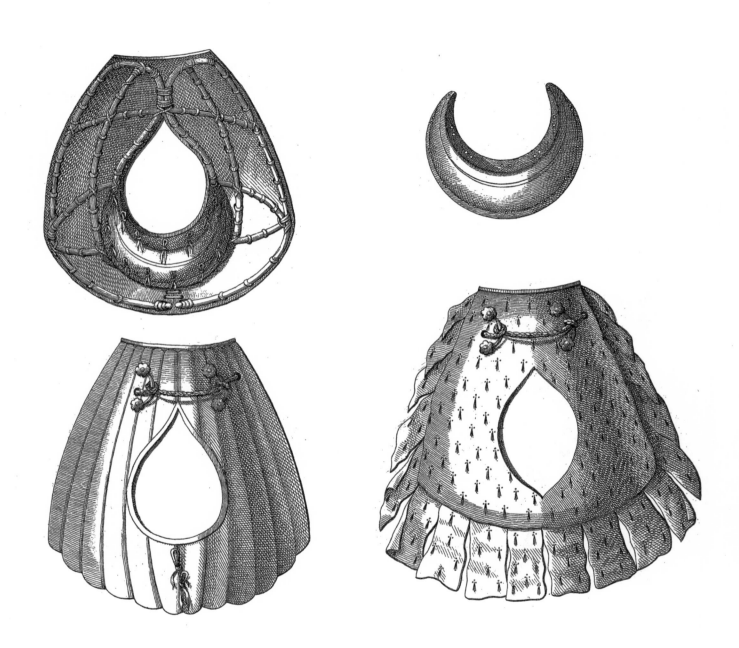

120   France

15th Century

Bardings for the joust. [*These horse armor, ordinarily covered by the peytrals and caparison, served not only to protect the horse's chest from frontal blows, but also to afford protection for the knight's legs. This type was attached to the front saddle-bow, and also provided the knight with a point of support for his left hand by means of a hemp or metal crosspiece. It was stuffed with straw and reinforced underneath with osier rods.*]

121 *France*

15th Century

Anne of Brittany.

Sources: Codex in the Bibliothèque Nationale, Paris; De Witt.

122 *France*

15th Century

Masculine and feminine dress.

Source: Painting, "Foundation of the Church of Sts. Peter and Paul," in Rheims; reproduced in Lacroix.

123   *France*

15th Century

Jean de Montague, "Grand maitre de France," Louis II, Duke of Bourbon, and other personages of the French Court (1400–1420).

Sources: Jacquemin; Montfaucon; Planché.

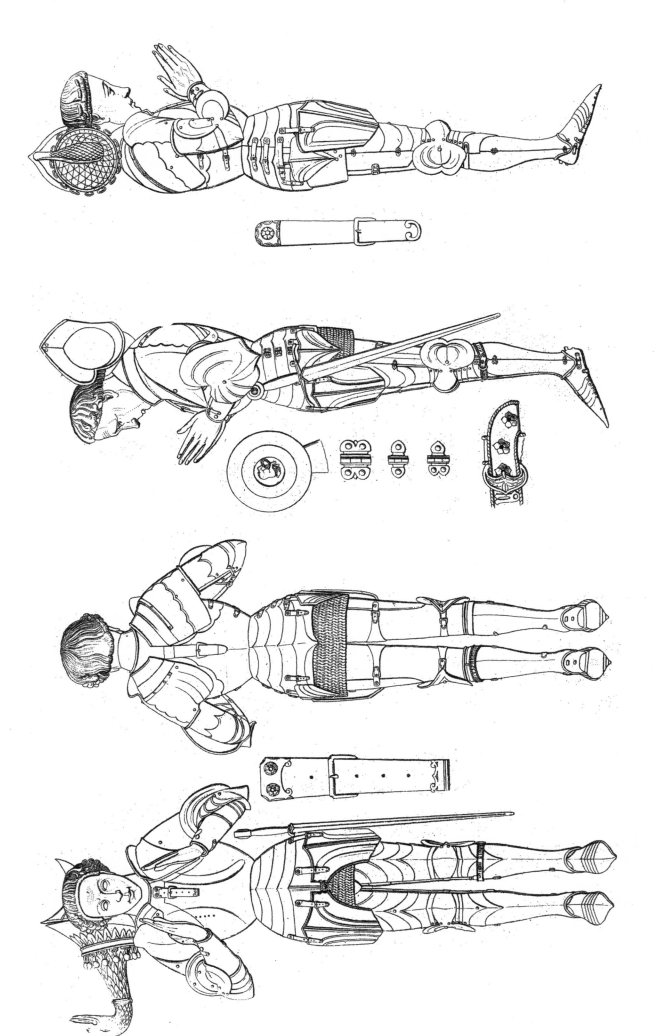

124　England

15th Century

Plated armor for a knight.

Source:　The effigy of Richard Beauchamp, Earl of Warwick (d. 1439), in the Church of St. Mary, Warwick.

125 *England*

15th Century

Dress and hairstyles.

Source: Sculptures on the tomb of Richard Beauchamp, Earl of Warwick, in the Church of St. Mary, Warwick.

126 *Flanders*

15th Century

Dress and hairstyles.

Source: Miniature in the Grimani Breviary, in the Biblioteca Marciana, Venice.

127 *Flanders*

15th Century

Pierantonio Baroncelli and his wife Maria Bonciani, in Flemish dress.

Source: Painting by an unknown Flemish artist, in the Gallery of the Uffizi, Florence.

128   *The Netherlands*

15th Century

Group of knights.

Source: The polyptych by Hubert and Jan Van Eyck, in Ghent.

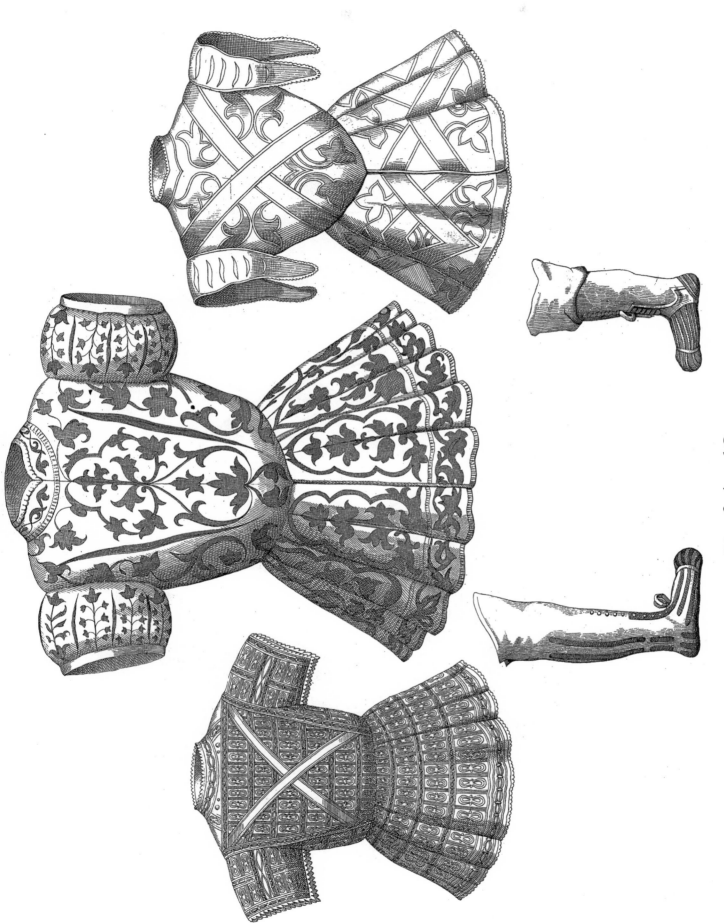

129   *Spain and Germany*
15th Century

Dress and footwear.

Sources: Documents preserved in the Royal Armory, Madrid.

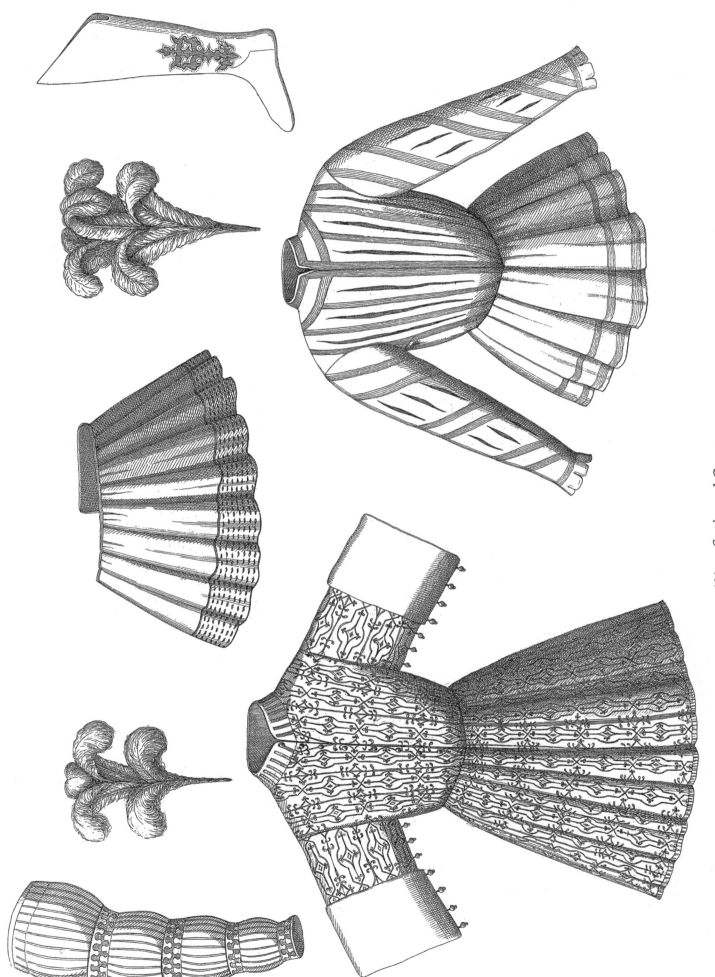

130   *Spain and Germany*
15th Century (end)
Dress and footwear.

Sources: Documents preserved in the Royal Armory, Madrid.

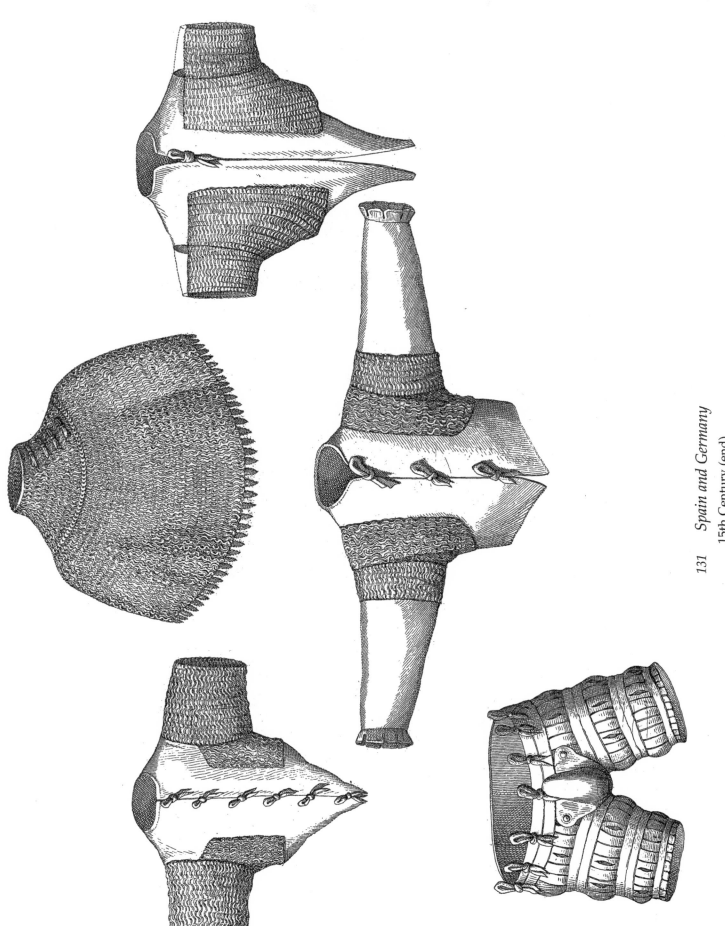

131   *Spain and Germany*

15th Century (end)

Details of leather and mail jerkins.

Sources: Drawings taken from documents preserved in the Royal Armory, Madrid.

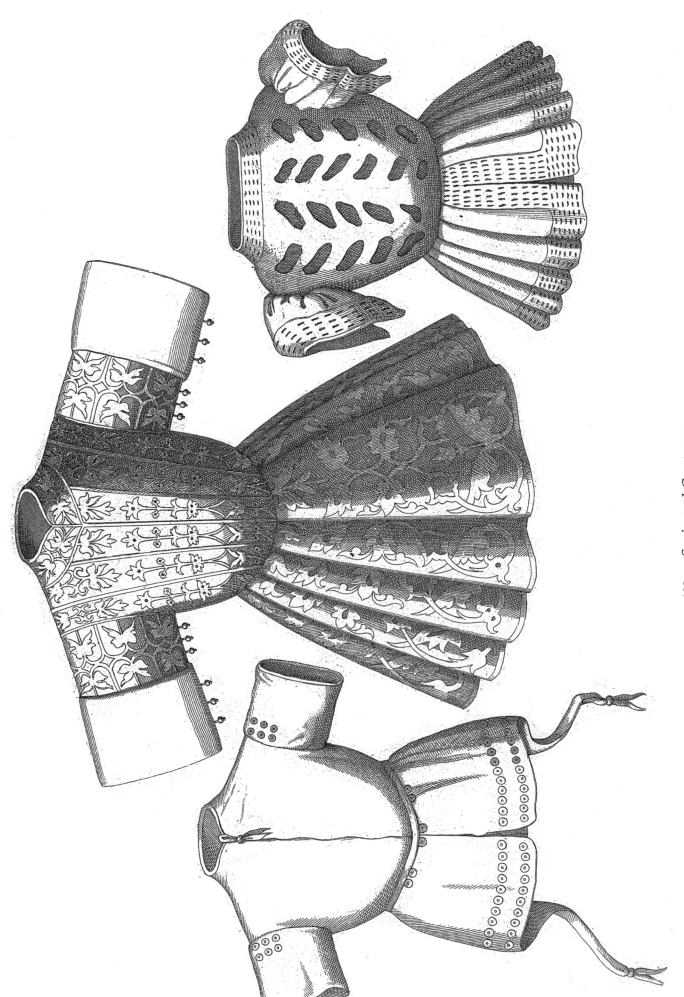

132 *Spain and Germany*
15th Century (end)
Herald's coat of arms.

Sources: Drawings taken from documents preserved in the Royal Armory, Madrid.

133 *Turkey*

15th Century (end)

Dress and styles.

Sources: Paintings by Vittore Carpaccio, in the Church of S. Giorgio degli Schiavoni, Venice.

134 *Turkey*

15th Century

Dress and styles.

Sources: Paintings by Vittore Carpaccio, in the Church of S. Giorgia degli Schiavoni, Venice.

135 *Italy*

15th Century

Cuirass and helmet in "classical style," with embossed and chiselled ornamentation.

Source: The Artillery Museum (now Musée de l'Armée), Paris.

136   Italy

16th Century

Equestrian armor of the second half of the 16th century. [*This armor, in the Royal Armory, Turin, was erroneously attributed to Antonio I Martinengo.*]

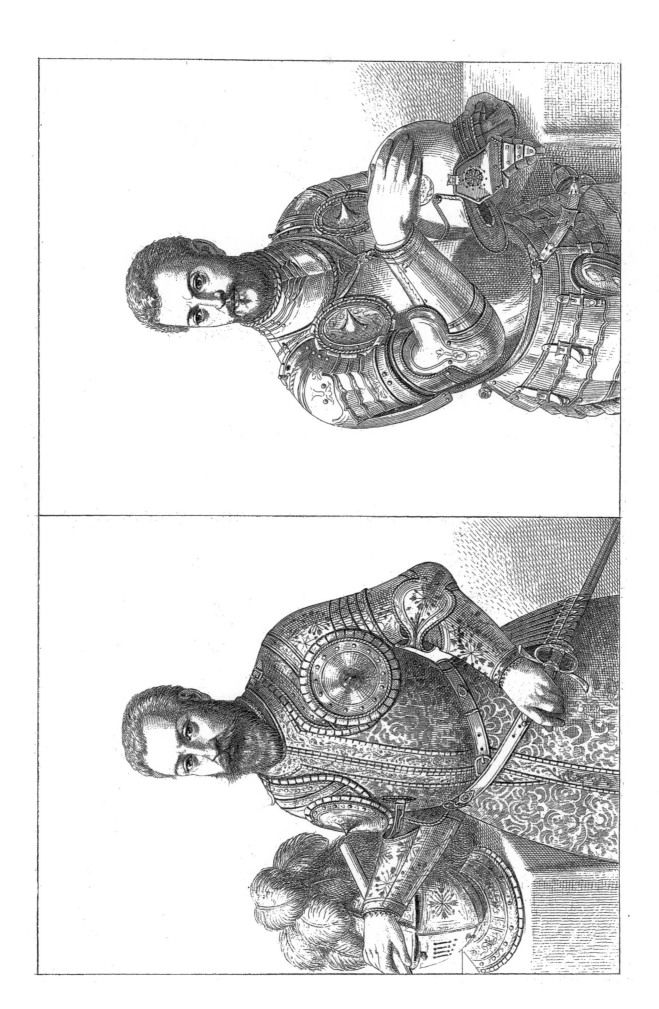

137 *Italy*
16th Century
Parade armor.

Sources: 1 Unidentified portrait in the Stibbert Museum. 2 Portrait of Cosimo I de' Medici, by A. Bronzino, in the Pitti Palace.

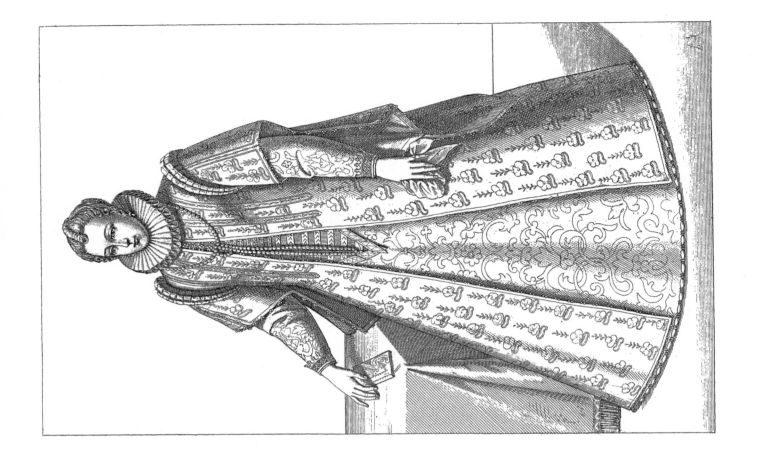

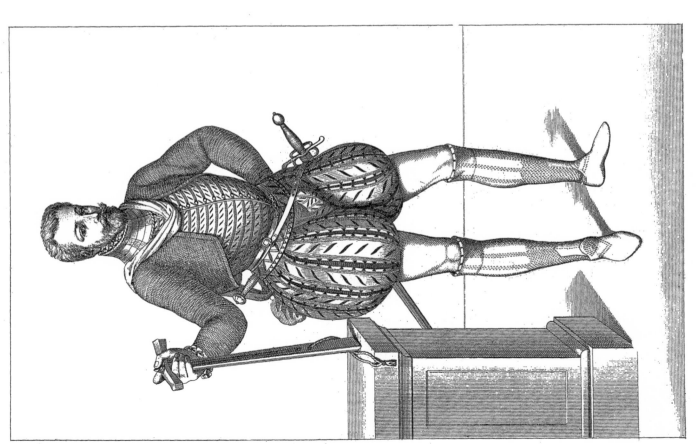

138 *Italy*
16th Century

1 Alfonso d'Este, Duke of Ferrara (1533–1597). 2 Eleonora d'Este, sister of Alfonso, Duke of Ferrara.

Sources: Colored engravings by Gregorio Cleter and Franco Cairoli, after contemporary portraits.

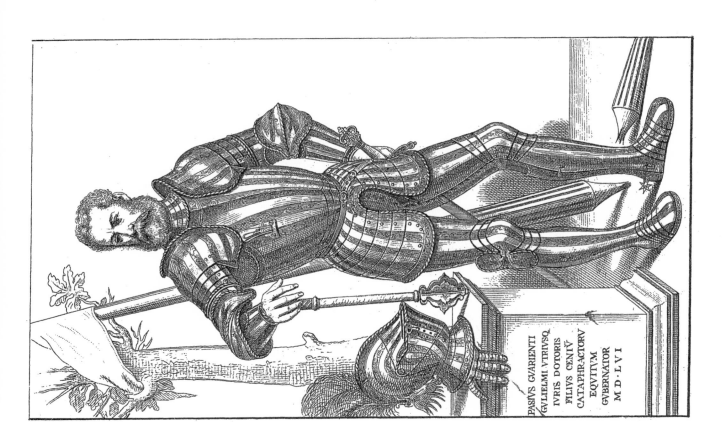

139   Italy

16th Century

1 Pace Guarienti. 2 Duke Alessandro de' Medici.

Sources: 1 Painting by Paolo Veronese, in the Galleria Comunale, Verona. 2 Portrait, with various additions, in the Uffizi Gallery.

140   *Italy*

16th Century

Guidobaldo II, Duke of Urbino.

Source: Painting by A. Bronzino, with legs added, in the Pitti Palace.

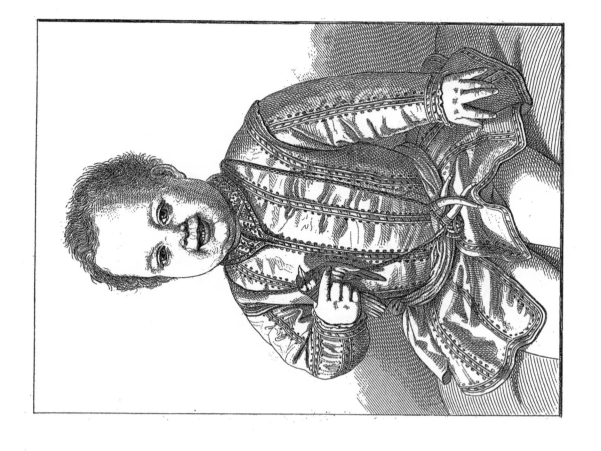

141 *Italy*

16th Century

Clothing for infants.

Sources: 1 Portrait in the Stibbert Museum. 2 Portrait of Don Garzia de' Medici, by Bronzino, in the Pitti Palace.

142 *Italy*
16th Century

Venetian dress and hairstyles. [*The first figure is said to represent a "rich courtesan in winter dress"; the second, a "noble debutante."*]

Source: Franco.

143 *Italy*

16th Century

Young Venetian in elegant dress.

Source: Franco.

144   Italy

16th Century (end)

1, 2 Venetian dress of the end of the 16th century. 3, 4 A foreign merchant and a
Venetian lady.

Source: Franco.

145   *Italy*
16th Century (end)
Feminine hairstyles.

Source: Portraits in the Uffizi Gallery.

146   *Germany*

16th Century (beginning)

Emperor Maximilian I.

Source: Painting by Peter Paul Rubens, in the Imperial Gallery, Vienna.

147 *Germany*

16th Century (first half)

Herr Wolfgang von Polheim, jousting master of Maximilian I.

Source: Note: *Stibbert attributed this drawing and the ones up to Plate 153 to the* Triumph of Maximilian, *a series of 134 large woodcuts showing the magnificent displays at Court, the majordomos, huntsmen, singers, instrumentalists, and standard-bearers of the Emperor. Actually, the drawings are from another series known as "Burgkmair's Tournament Book," which is very closely allied with that artist's woodcuts for the Triumph of Maximilian.*

148   Germany

16th Century (first half)

Jousters on foot, in complete armor and with armets instead of helms. [*They are armed with swords and tilting lances, in the manner of mounted jousters, but the lances do not have vamplates.*]

Source: See Note, Plate 147.

149 *Germany*

16th Century (first half)

Knights armed for the "Giostra della coda" (Course à la queue). [*In this course, the knight's shield, covered with a piece of fabric, was so attached that it would fly up into the air, given a direct hit by the lance. The horses were blindfolded.*]

Source: See Note, Plate 147.

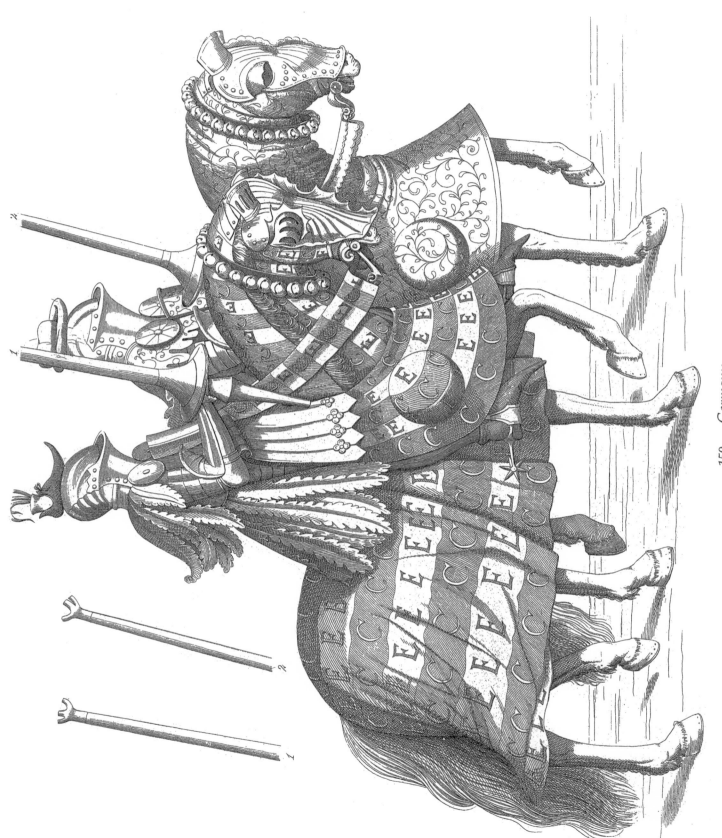

150 Germany
16th Century (first half)

Knights armed for the joust "à la haute barde."

Source: See Note, Plate 147.

151 *Germany*

16th Century (first half)

Knights armed for the joust "à la targe futée." [*In this joust, a blow of the lance, if well directed, would cause a metal plate fixed to the breastplate and attached to a spring, to fly off in pieces.*]

Source: See Note, Plate 147.

152 *Germany*
16th Century (first half)

Knights armed for the "Giostra all'italiana" (Italian joust).

Source: See Note, Plate 147.

153 *Germany*

16th Century (first half)

Knights armed for the field course.

Source: See Note, Plate 147.

154   *Germany*
16th Century

Armor and bardings for tournaments and jousts of the first half of the 16th century.

Source: The "Tournament Book of Duke William IV of Bavaria, from 1510 to 1545."

155 *Germany*
16th Century

Armor and bardings for tournaments and jousts of the first half of the 16th century.

Source: The "Tournament Book of Duke William IV of Bavaria, from 1510 to 1545."

156   Germany

16th Century

Armor and bardings for tournaments and jousts of the first half of the 16th century.

Source: The "Tournament Book of Duke William IV of Bavaria, from 1510 to 1545."

157   Germany

16th Century

Armor and bardings for tournaments and jousts of the first half of the 16th century.

Source: The "Tournament Book of Duke William IV of Bavaria, from 1510 to 1545."

158 *Germany*

16th Century

Armor and bardings for tournaments and jousts of the first half of the 16th century.

Source: The "Tournament Book of Duke William IV of Bavaria, from 1510 to 1545."

159　*Germany*

16th Century

Armor and bardings for tournaments and jousts of the first half of the 16th century.

Source:　The "Tournament Book of Duke William IV of Bavaria, from 1510 to 1545."

160   *Germany*

16th Century

Armor and bardings for tournaments and jousts of the first half of the 16th century.

Source: The "Tournament Book of Duke William IV of Bavaria, from 1510 to 1545."

161   *Germany*

16th Century

Armor and bardings for tournaments and jousts of the first half of the 16th century.

Source: The "Tournament Book of Duke William IV of Bavaria, from 1510 to 1545."

162   Germany

16th Century

Armor and bardings for tournaments and jousts of the first half of the 16th century.

Source: The "Tournament Book of Duke William IV of Bavaria, from 1510 to 1545."

163   Germany

16th Century

Armor and bardings for tournaments and jousts of the first half of the 16th century.

Source: The "Tournament Book of Duke William IV of Bavaria, from 1510 to 1545."

164   Germany

16th Century

Armor and bardings for tournaments and jousts of the first half of the 16th century.

Source: The "Tournament Book of Duke William IV of Bavaria, from 1510 to 1545."

165 *Germany*
16th Century

Armor and bardings for tournaments and jousts of the first half of the 16th century.

Source: The "Tournament Book of Duke William IV of Bavaria, from 1510 to 1545."

166   *Germany*

16th Century

Parade armor. [*This armor, preserved in the Dresden Museum, belonged to Christian II, Elector of Saxony.*]

167   Germany

16th Century

Armor of the second half of the 16th century. [*This armor, preserved in the Dresden Museum, belonged to Christian I, Elector of Saxony.*]

168   Germany

16th Century

Mounted man at arms.

Source: Albrecht Dürer's engraving, "The Knight, Death, and the Devil."

169   Germany

16th Century (beginning)

Full equestrian armor of Augustus I, Elector of Saxony (1526–1586).

Source: The Museum of Dresden.

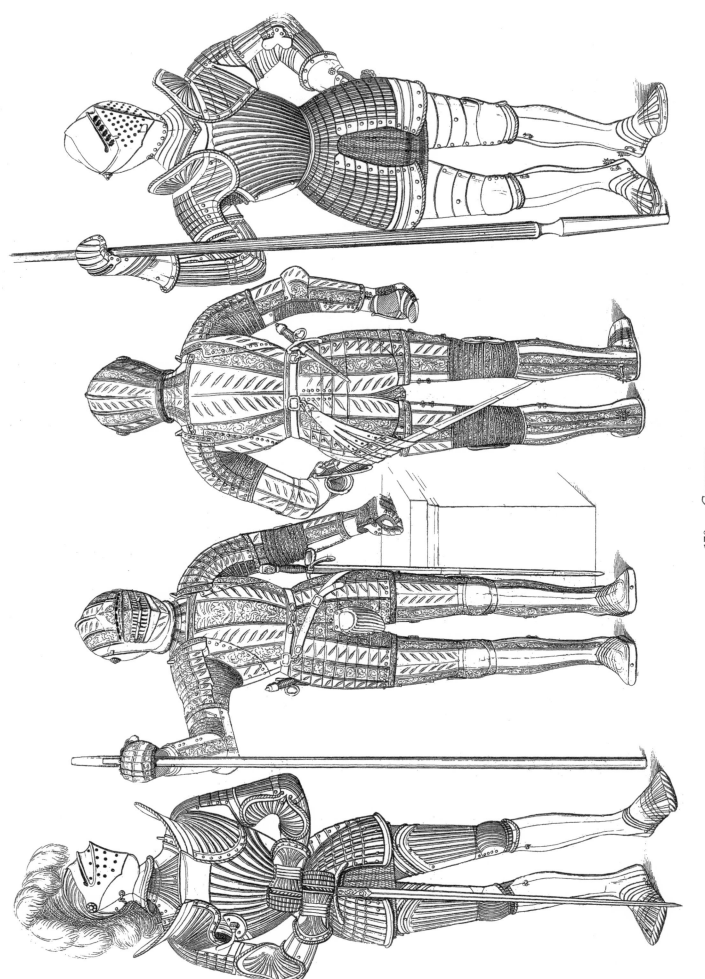

170　*Germany*

16th Century (beginning)

1, 4 Fluted or "Maximilian" armor, preserved in the Hermitage Museum. 2, 3 Armor for foot combat, preserved in the Musée de l'Armée, Paris.

171 *Germany*

16th Century (first half)

1, 2 Foot soldiers. 3, 4, 5 Knights.

Sources: 1, 2 Contemporary engravings, artists unknown. 3–5 Illustration by Hans Burgkmair in "Der Weisskunig."

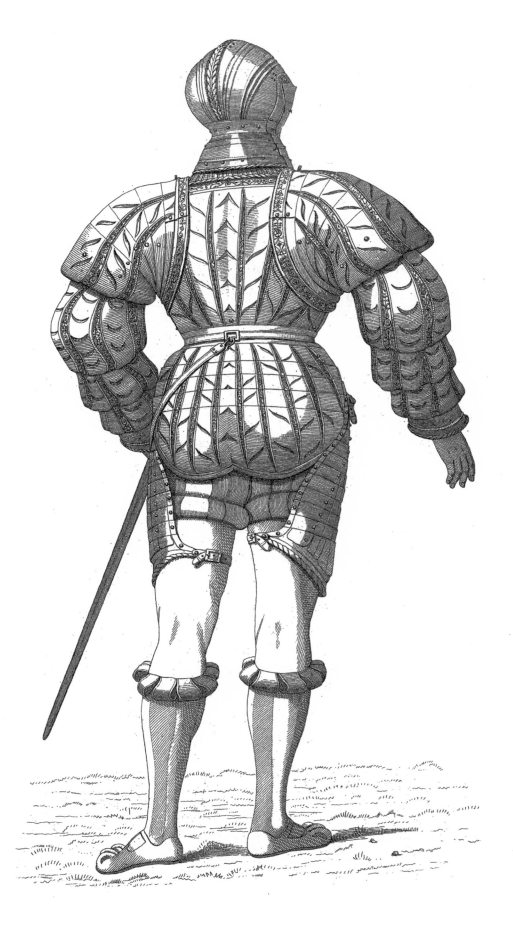

172 *Germany*

16th Century (first half)

Armor and military styles. [*Armor of this kind was intended for foot combat and was designed to imitate closely civilian dress of the time of Emperor Maximilian I. The puffs and slashes of the doublet and trunk-hose are reproduced on the arm defenses, the breastplate, and on the cuisses.*]

173 *Germany*

16th Century (first half)

Armor and military style. [*This armor, preserved in the Kunsthistorisches Museum, Vienna, belonged to Wilhelm von Roggendorf, one of the captains who defended Vienna against the Turks in 1529.*]

174   *Germany*

16th Century (first half)

Armor and feminine dress.

Sources: 2 The "Judgment of Paris," by Lucas Cranach. 1, 3, 4 Pen drawings, colored in India inks,
by Hans Holbein.

175   *Germany*
16th Century (first half)
Foot soldiers.

Sources: Contemporary engravings by Hans Baldung Grün and Daniel Hopfer.

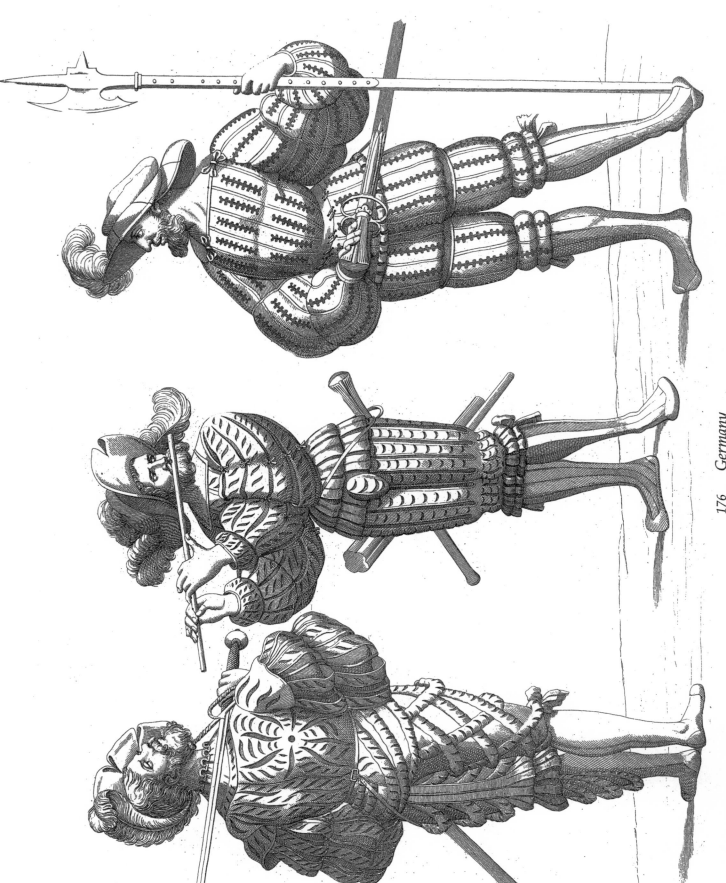

176 *Germany*
16th Century
Foot soldiers.

Sources: Contemporary prints by Daniel Hopfer.

177 *Germany*
16th Century (first half)

1 A lady of Bale. 2 Armor in the Kunsthistorisches Museum, Vienna. 3 Johann Friedrich, Elector of Saxony. 4, 5 Foot soldiers.

Sources: 1 Pen drawings by Hans Holbein. 3 Engraving by Lucas Cranach. 4, 5 Contemporary prints, artists unknown.

178   Germany

16th Century (first half)

Foot soldiers.

Sources: Contemporary prints, artists unknown.

179 *Germany*
16th Century (first half)
Foot soldiers.

Sources: Contemporary prints, artists unknown.

180 *Germany*
16th Century (first half)
Foot soldiers.

Sources: Contemporary prints, artists unknown.

181 *Germany*
16th Century

Dress, weapons, and hairstyles of the first half of the 16th century.

Source: The engravings of Albrecht Dürer.

182   *Germany*

16th Century (beginning)

Feminine dress.

Source: Painting by Hans Suess von Kolmbach, in the Uffizi Gallery.

183 *Germany*

16th Century

Noble and burgher dress of the beginning of the 16th century.

Sources: Engravings and drawings by Albrecht Dürer, and a painting by Hans Holbein (St. Sebastian, Munich).

184   *Germany*
16th Century

1, 4 The Burgormaster Meyer and his family. 2 Huntsman's outfit. 3 A gentlewoman.

Sources: 1, 4 Painting by Hans Holbein, in the Grandducal Palace, Darmstadt. 2 Albrecht Dürer's engraving "The Vision of St. Eustace."

185 Germany

16th Century (first half)

1 A lady of Basel. 2, 3, 4 Gentlewomen. 5 Commoner in travel dress.

Sources: 1 Drawing by Hans Holbein. 2, 3, 4 Contemporary prints and engravings, artists unknown. 5 Contemporary print, artist unknown.

186 *Germany*

16th Century

Feminine dress.

Source: Painting by Lucas Cranach.

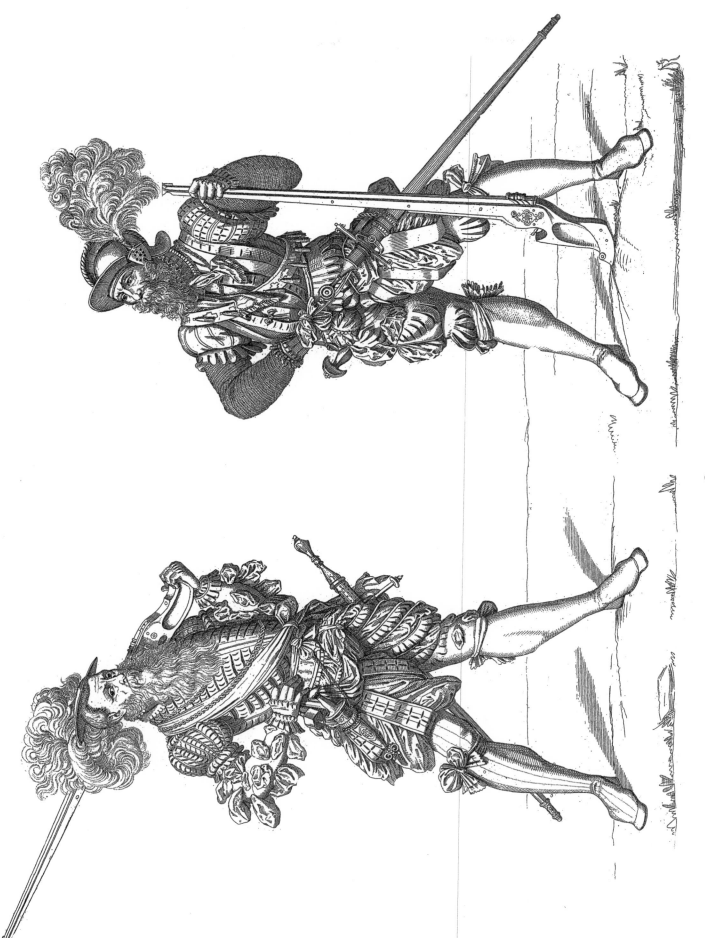

187   Germany
16th Century (second half)
Gunners.

Source: Stained glass window by Daniel Lindtmayer.

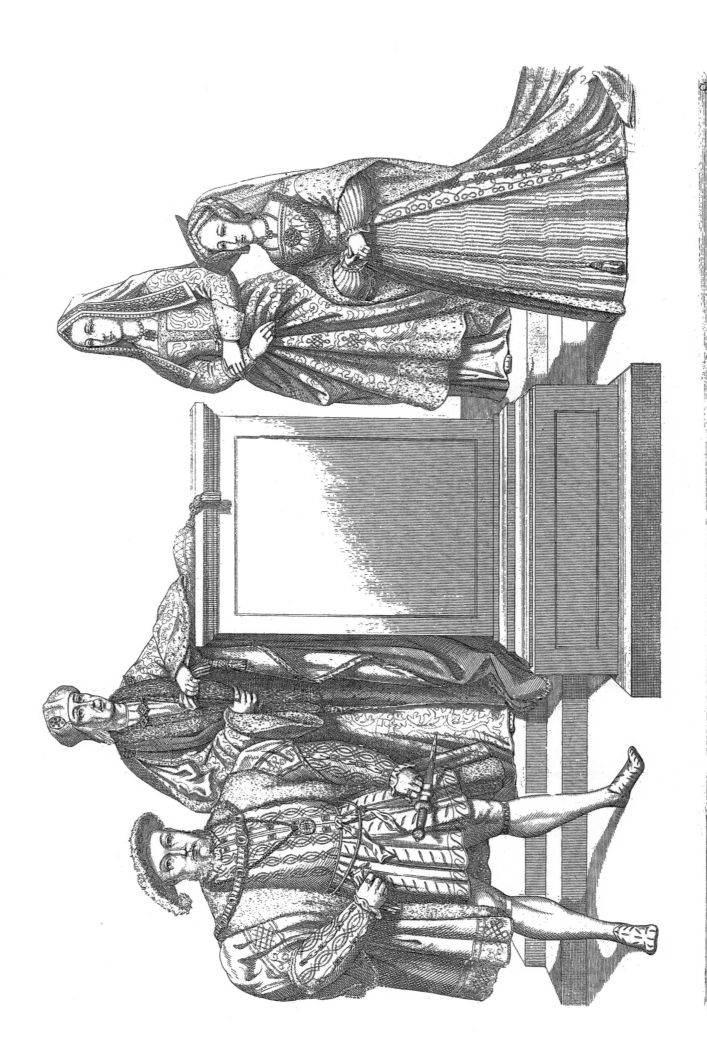

188   *England*

16th Century

The Royal Family, Henry VIII and Jane Seymour.

Source: Painting by Hans Holbein, in the Kensington Museum, London.

189   *England*

16th Century

Countess Anne of Cleves.

Source: Painting by Hans Holbein.

190   *England*
16th Century

Charles Brandon, Duke of Suffolk, and his wife Mary, widow of King Louis XII of France.

Source: Painting by Lucas de Heere.

191   *England*
16th Century

Sir Adrian Stokes, Esq., and his wife Frances, Duchess of Suffolk.

Source: Painting by Lucas de Heere.

The Netherlands
16th Century

The Counts of Holland and Flanders: 1 Theodoric of Aquitania. 2 John of Holland. 3 Maximilian of Austria. [*The figures of the nobles, up to that of Charles V, are represented in the dress and armor of the 15th and the beginning of the 16th century.*]

Source: Illustrations in the book "Effigies Comitum Hollandiae et Zelandiae."

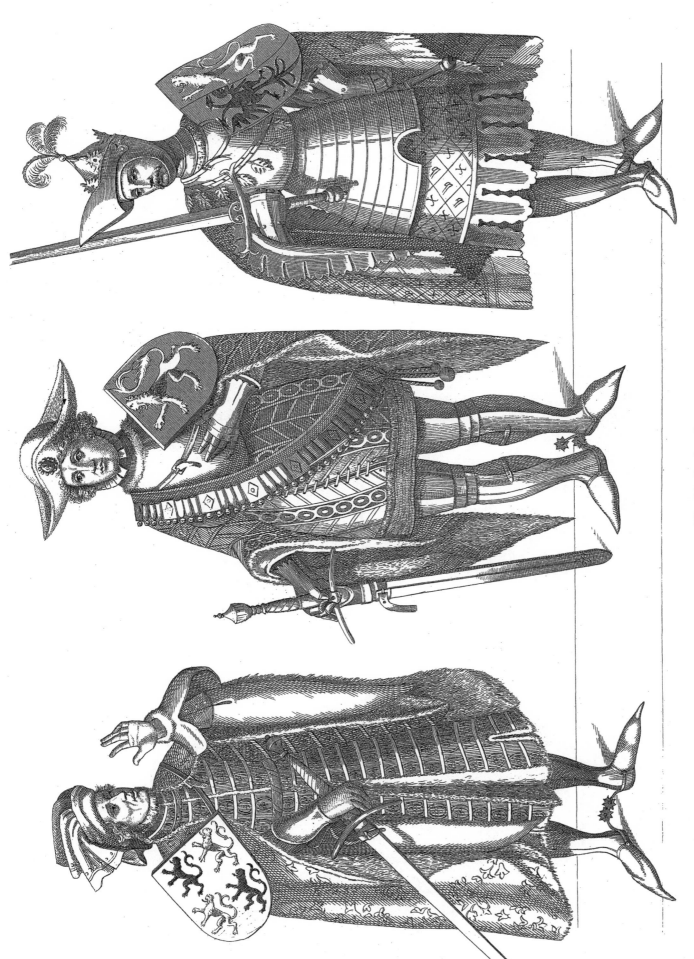

193 *The Netherlands*

16th Century

The Counts of Holland and Flanders: 1 William III. 2 Florenzio. 3 William II, King of the Romans.

Source: Illustrations in the book "Effigies Comitum Hollandiae et Zelandiae."

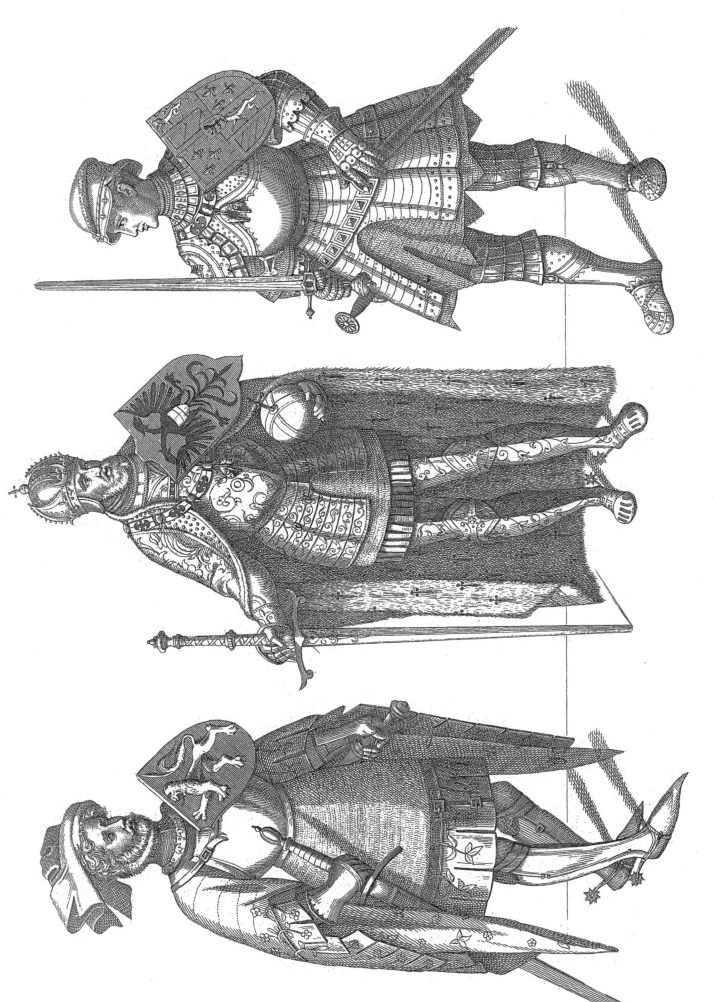

194   *The Netherlands*
16th Century

The Counts of Holland and Flanders: 1 Theodoric VII. 2 Charles V. 3 Charles of Burgundy.

Source: Illustrations in the book "Effigies Comitum Hollandiae et Zelandiae."

195　　*The Netherlands*
16th Century

The Counts of Holland and Flanders: 1 Ada, daughter of Theodoric VII. 2 Gertrude of Saxony. 3 Empress Margaret.

Source:　Illustrations in the book "Effigies Comitum Hollandiae et Zelandiae."

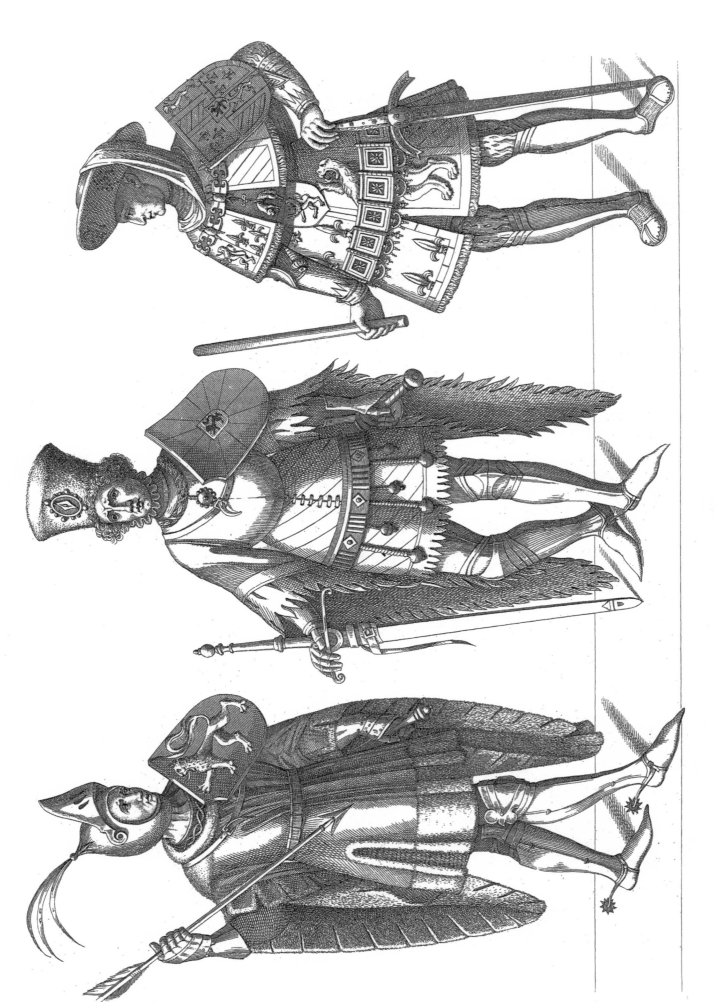

196 *The Netherlands*
16th Century

The Counts of Holland and Flanders: 1 Theodoric IV. 2 Robert the Phyrgian. 3 Philip the Good.

Source: Illustrations in the book "Effigies Comitum Hollandiae et Zelandiae."

197　*Spain*
16th Century

Armor and horse trappings.

Source:　A Brussels tapestry showing Charles V reviewing his militia, in the Royal Palace, Madrid.

198   *Spain*

16th Century

Don Juan of Austria, natural son of Charles V. [*The trunk-hose are padded with bombast, covered in silk, and over this are embroidered panes. The breastplate was in the peascod form, "à bosse de polichinelle," as the French called it, and followed the form of the doublets in fashion in the second half of the 16th century.*]

Source: Painting by an unknown artist, in the Prado, Madrid.

199   *Spain*

16th Century

A gentleman.

Source: Painting by Antonio Moro, in the Prado, Madrid.

200   *Spain*

16th Century

Infanta Isabella, daughter of Philip II.

Source: Painting by Coello (Alonzo Sanchez), in the Prado, Madrid.

201 *Italy*

17th Century (first half)

Prince Tommaso di Savoia-Carignano. [*By the beginning of the 17th century, suits of armor were already discarding certain pieces because perfected firearms made plate armor of the previous century inadequate. In addition, the plates "proved" by firearms were so heavy that gradually the less important pieces were discarded: the greaves were replaced by the leather boot, the gorget by the lace collar, and the helmet by the broad-brimmed felt hat, reinforced inside by a metal skullcap.*]

Source: Painting by Anthony Van Dyck, in the Turin Gallery.

202 *Italy*

17th Century

Captain's armor and horse trappings, first half of the 17th century. [*The Visconti arms appear on the breastplate and on the horse's harness.*]

Source: Painting by an unknown artist, in the Stibbert Museum.

203 *Italy*

17th Century

A Knight of Malta.

Source: Painting by an unknown artist, in the Stibbert Museum.

204 *Italy*
17th Century

A gentleman and women.

Sources: Paintings in the Stibbert Museum.

205 *Italy*

17th Century

Cammillo dei Marchesi del Monte S. Maria (Bourbon del Monte), Field Master at Milan
for the House of Austria, and General of the Infantry in Tuscany in 1638.

Source: Painting in the Stibbert Museum.

206 *Italy*
17th Century
Feminine dress.

Sources: Paintings in the Stibbert Museum.

207   *Italy*

17th Century

Duke Armand Frédéric of Schomberg, Marshal of France.

Source: Painting by Godfrey Kneller.

208   *Germany*

17th Century (first half)

Gunner.

Source: Print by Hendrick Goltzius.

209 *Holland*

17th Century

Rembrandt's wife, Saskia van Vylenburgh.

Source: Painting by Rembrandt in the Gallery of Cassel.

210 *Holland*

17th Century

A gentleman.

Source: Painting by Gerard Terborch, in the National Gallery, London.

211 *Holland*

17th Century (second half)

Gentlemen in hunting dress.

Source: Abraham Hondius' painting "Boar Hunt," Rotterdam.

212   *Spain*

17th Century

Queen Margarita of Austria, wife of Philip III.

Source: Painting by Velasquez, in the Prado, Madrid.

213   *Spain*

17th Century

Queen Isabel of Bourbon, wife of Philip IV.

Source: Painting by Velasquez, in the Prado, Madrid.

214   *Spain*

17th Century

Infanta Maria Teresa, daughter of Philip IV, King of Spain. [*The Infanta wears the farthingale (guard infante) in vogue in the first half of the 17th century.*]

Source: Painting by Velasquez, in the Prado, Madrid.

215   *Germany*
18th Century

Feminine dress and hairstyles.

Sources: Contemporary prints.

216 *France*
18th Century (second half)
Feminine hairstyles.

Sources: Contemporary prints.

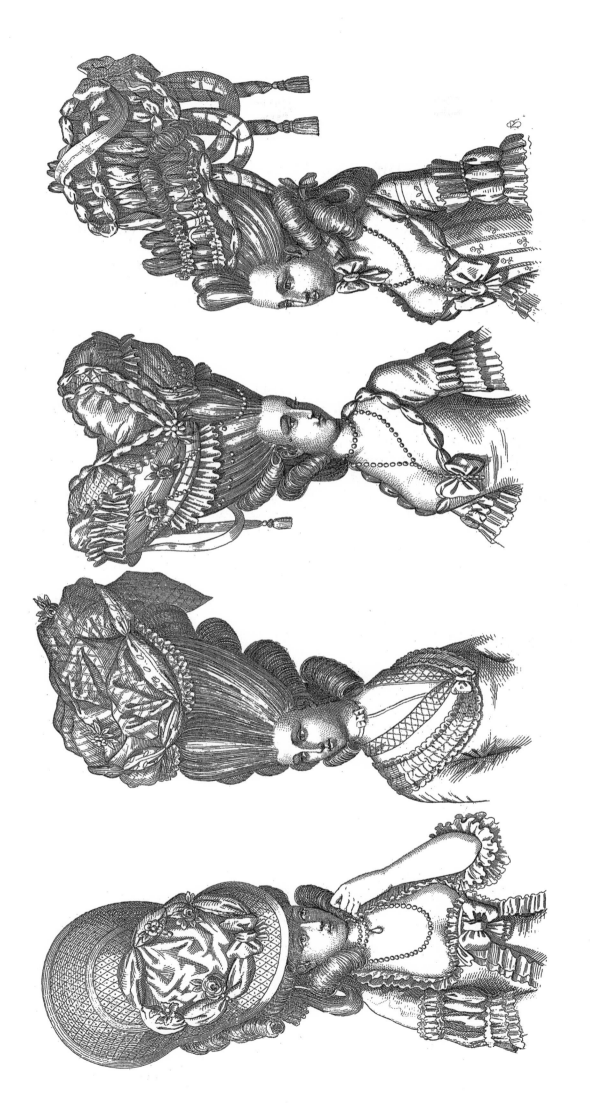

217 *France*
18th Century (second half)
Feminine hairstyles.

Sources: Contemporary prints.

BIBLIOGRAPHY

Bar, Jacques Charles. *Recueil de tous les costumes religieux et militaires.* Paris, 1778.

De Witt, M. *Chroniqueurs de l'Histoire de France.* Paris, 1886.

Franco, Giacomo. *Habiti delle donne venetiane intagliate in rame nuovamente.* Venice, 1610.

Hefner-Alteneck, J. H. von. *Costume du moyen-âge chrétien.* Mannheim, 1860.

Hefner-Alteneck, J. H. von. *Trachten, Kunstwerke und Geräthschaften vom frühen Mittelalter bis Ende des achtzehnten Jahrhunderts nach gleichzeitigen Originalen.* Frankfurt, 1879.

Hottenroth, Freidrich von. *Trachten, Haus-, Feld-, und Kriegsgeräthschaften der Völker alter und neuer Zeit.* Stuttgart, 1884.

Jacquemin, Raphael. *Iconographie générale et méthodique du Costume du IVe au XIXe siècle.* Paris, 1869.

Kretschmer, Albert. *The Book of Costumes.*

Lacroix, Paul. *Le Moyen-Age et la Renaissance.* Paris, 1849.

Meyrick, Samuel Rush. *Antient Armour as it Existed in Europe, but particularly in England.* London, 1824.

Meyrick, Samuel Rush, and Smith, Charles Hamilton. *The Costume of the Original Inhabitants of the British Islands.* London, 1815.

Montfaucon, Bernard de. *Les monumens de la Monarchie françois.* Paris, 1733.

Planché, James Robinson. *A Cyclopedia of Costume or Dictionary of Dress.* London, 1876.

Shaw, Henry. *Dresses and Decoration of the Middle Ages.* London, 1858.

Strutt, Joseph. *The Manners and Customs of the Antient Britons from the Arrival of Julius Caesar until the Saxon Conquest.* London, 1775.

Tournament Book of Duke William IV of Bavaria, from 1510 to 1545. Munich: Frederick Schlichtegroll, 1817.

Viollet-le-Duc, Eugene Emmanuel. *Dictionnaire raissoné du mobilier français de l'epoque carlovingienne à la Renaissance.* Paris, 1875.

Willemin, Nicholas Xavier. *Monuments français inedits.* 1825–39.